DEDICATION

To our mothers,
Mary Barton Robinson and Inez Wilcox Hillman,
both dedicated athletes, who nurtured our love of sports.

FOREWORD

Sports has given more to me than I ever dreamed possible. Basketball enabled me to play on two national championship teams, win an Olympic medal, become a basketball Hall of Famer, commentate on network television, coach in the WNBA, and meet my husband, Tim.

But athletic involvement brought me something greater than all these accomplishments. My Olympic teammate Nancy Dunkle and Athletes in Action's Ralph Drollinger taught me to know Jesus Christ.

Twenty years later, Athletes in Action offered me an opportunity to repay this debt and revive my basketball career. In 1996 at age 37, I accepted an invitation to join the organization's national touring women's team.

The decision meant leaving my family and attending a six-week training camp. But sharing a spiritual environment and bonding with sister Christian athletes made the absence worthwhile.

The experience provided an added dividend. Playing a rigorous schedule against collegiate competition showcased my basketball skills. Without the Athletes in Action exposure, the WBNA would never have granted me a tryout.

These events didn't occur by chance. God's hand directed them as He has my entire life.

Raised in a non-Christian environment, God's direction wasn't always apparent. Hundreds of questions had to be answered before I began to walk in His way, and even then, every day represented a challenge to my faith.

Just as athletes cannot hone their skills and succeed without playbooks and training manuals, Christians cannot tune their lives into proper focus without strong devotional materials. For me, nothing enriches more than reading about real people and how they handle life's complexities.

Devotions from the World of Women's Sports connects stories of female competitors with insightful spiritual applications. Spending a few minutes each day with one of these devotions reminds Christians that life's goal shouldn't be convenience but rather commitment.

Kathy and John Hillman serve a long-neglected need though *Devotions from the World of Women's Sports.* Their book highlights women's athletic achievements from a Christian point of view. Too often, our gender has been mentioned only as an afterthought or filler.

Women of all ages, both athletes and nonathletes, can learn valuable lessons from these outstanding female achievers. Many names come straight from today's headlines. Others have been buried for years in obscurity. But these stories don't just entertain. They enlighten, educate, and inspire.

As a player and coach, I serve as role model and instructor. As a believer, I strive to grow closer to God, and as a mother, I teach my son T.J. to honor Him.

Devotions from the World of Women's Sports meets each of these needs.

Nancy Lieberman-Cline
General Manager/Coach, Detroit Shock

LOOK FOR THESE SPECIAL FEATURES . . .

 **From the Playbook**—A key Scripture from God's Word.

 **From the Pressbox**—Glimpses from the pages of sports history and how we can see God's principles at work in the world around us.

 **From the Coach**—An action point or activity that will demonstrate to us personally our need to follow God, and show us how we can be a winner if we "practice" being like Him.

WOMEN'S BASKETBALL MAKES THE OLYMPICS

Therefore, if anyone is in Christ, he is a new creation; the old has gone, the new has come!

—2 CORINTHIANS 5:17

The International Olympic Committee added women's basketball as a competitive sport to the 1976 summer games. Six countries—Bulgaria, Canada, Czechoslovakia, Japan, the Soviet Union, and the United States—vied for the first gold medal.

The Soviets entered the competition as heavy favorites. Paced by the 6-foot-10^3/$_4$-inch center, Iuliyaka Semenova, the team had not lost a game in five years and had been undefeated in international competition since 1958.

The American squad consisted of an assortment of amateurs and collegians such as Lusia Harris of Delta State, University of California at Los Angeles' Ann Meyers, Nancy Lieberman, future star at Old Dominion, and Pat Head (Summit), a graduate of the University of Tennessee at Martin. Given the embryonic state of women's basketball in the United States, few expected the Americans to make a major impact at the Olympics.

The U.S.A. team suffered an immediate setback, losing to Japan, 84–71. Four of the five Japanese starters played the entire 40 minutes with Keiko Namai scoring 35 points.

The young American squad rebounded with wins over Bulgaria, 95–79, and Canada, 89–75. Nancy Dunkle, Patricia Roberts, and Ann Meyers led a balanced attack over the Bulgarians, scoring 17, 16, and 15 points. Dunkle's 15 and Juliene Simpson's 14 points spearheaded the victory over the Canadians.

The Soviet Union loomed next. A crowd of nearly 5,000 jammed the Montreal Olympic arena, most hoping for an American upset. But the taller Russians dominated from the start, jumping to a 15–0 lead. Semenova led the way with 20 first-half points. She played little in the second half but still finished the game with 32. The Soviet Union coasted to a 112–77 victory.

The United States amateurs refused to let the crushing defeat dampen their spirits. In their final contest against Czechoslovakia, the Americans erupted from a 37–37 halftime tie to outscore the Czechs, 46–30 in the second half.

The 83–67 triumph brought the United States basketball team a silver medal and served notice to all the world that the American women would always be competitive and top contenders.

In 1976, women's basketball became a new Olympic sport. American women were relatively new to full-court women's basketball. In fact, women's team sports had just begun to emerge at competitive levels on the college scene in the United States. A new day had dawned for female athletes.

Women's basketball began opening doors to college scholarships, opportunities for Olympic and international competition, and respect for females in sport. The old attitudes departed. The new arrived.

Salvation through Christ also brings a new day for those who choose to trust Him. Former ways begin to disappear as God's love and righteousness push out sin and selfishness. The old self has gone. The new creation has come.

List as many women's basketball players as you can who played in 1976 or earlier. How did you do? If you didn't do well, list as many women athletes as you can who competed in or before 1976. Thank God for new things He brings in life. Praise Him for the newness He gives through salvation.

NANCY LIEBERMAN-CLINE LIVES HER DREAM

"Here comes that dreamer!" They said to each other.
—GENESIS 37:19

By the time Nancy Lieberman reached age 14, she had logged thousands of hours playing pickup basketball. As a young girl in Queens, New York, she engaged any and all challengers on the court, often shooting late into the evening under streetlights.

Nancy dreamed that someday basketball would provide her with the same opportunities it provided men. She idolized the New York Knickerbockers and selected Willis Reed, Dave Debusschere, and Walt Frazier as her role models.

But her mother had other ideas. She pleaded with her daughter to forget basketball and concentrate on a more traditional occupation. One day in frustration, she punctured Nancy's basketball with a screwdriver.

The teenager refused to buckle. After graduating from Far Rockaway High School in 1976, she earned a spot on the first United States women's Olympic basketball team and claimed a silver medal.

Four years at Old Dominion University brought further accolades. The three-time All-American led the Lady Monarchs to a 72–2 record and two national championships. Lieberman scored 2,430 points, pulled down 1,167 rebounds, and collected 961 assists. Nancy twice won the Wade Trophy as National Player of the Year.

But life after college graduation offered limited chances to play the game she loved. Over the next seventeen years, the New York native performed in both women's and men's leagues for six different teams ranging from the Dallas Diamonds, Long Island Knights, and Washington Generals to Athletes in Action.

In 1997, Nancy Lieberman-Cline received the chance of a lifetime. A new women's professional league, the WNBA, formed, and the 38 year old signed with the Phoenix Mercury.

More than 16,000 fans packed the America West Arena for the Mercury's opener against the Charlotte Sting. Despite competing with and against women almost half her age, Nancy performed like a seasoned pro. She logged 21 minutes and hit 3-of-8 from the floor, scoring 8 points, grabbing 5 rebounds, and making 5 assists. Bridget Pettis paced the team with 17 points as the Mercury won handily, 76–59.

After the inaugural season, Nancy realized the time had come to step off the court. She didn't move very far as she entered the coach's box as the new head of the Detroit Shock.

Young Nancy Lieberman dreamed the dream of becoming a world-class basketball player. She dreamed of national championships, Olympic medals, professional teams, and supporting herself playing the game she loved.

Her mother tried to puncture her dream. Many wouldn't believe a woman could possibly fulfill such aspirations. It just didn't seem likely. Other than teaching physical education or coaching in a secondary school or maybe a college, making a living with basketball just wasn't possible.

But Nancy kept on. God had given her a dream, and it came true.

In the Bible, another teenager had dreams. His brothers tried to puncture his too but they couldn't. Instead Joseph kept on. God had provided the dreams, and they came true.

Read about Joseph's dreams in Genesis 37, 40–41. What are your dreams? Have they come from God? Think about what it will take to realize them. Are you willing? Ask your Heavenly Father to help you.

O Lord, when you favored me, you made my mountain stand firm. —PSALM 30:7

Bad luck haunted skier Picabo Street, and winning often eluded her. In the 1998 Nagano (Japan) Winter Olympics, experts considered the American more of a has-been than a medal contender. In December 1996, the racer had reached top form. But serious injuries suffered in a training run stopped the 1994 Olympic downhill silver medalist cold in her tracks.

Picabo spent months rehabilitating a torn left knee ligament, a ripped calf muscle, and a cracked femur. She missed the first few weeks of the 1997–98 European downhill season and finished in the top ten only once in eight races.

Another high-speed fall threatened her career. The mishap knocked the 26 year old unconscious and left her with a sore neck, but the accident also renewed Street's sense of purpose.

In the 1998 Olympic women's super giant slalom, the American drew the number two spot, normally an unfavorable position. She skied the course aggressively, taking chance after chance and finished in a time of 1:18.02.

As the day wore on, the times increased. Pre-race favorite, Germany's Katja Selzinger, turned in a time of 1:18.44, .42 seconds slower than Street. Only a dark horse came close to passing Picabo's clocking. Austrian Michaela Dorfmeister, competing in the 18th slot, completed her run in 1:18.03, a mere .01 second more than Street.

After 41 skiers raced the downhill slope, the Sun Valley, Idaho native's time ranked number one. The Olympic hopeful had finally captured gold.

Jean-Claude Killy, the hero of the 1968 Grenoble (France) Games, presented Picabo her medal and placed his hands on her

cheeks. She closed her eyes and clasped the symbol of her victory in both hands.

The 10-year skiing veteran sang the Star Spangled Banner with emotion. When the final note sounded, she brandished her floral bouquet, pumped her fist into the air, and blew a kiss to the crowd as she wiped away a tear.

Picabo Street had experienced bad luck after bad luck after bad luck. She survived injury after injury after injury. She spent countless hours in physical therapy and rehabilitation. She must have wondered if she would ever stay healthy. She surely questioned whether she would ever reach her potential. The skier even drew one of the poorest spots in the Olympic super giant slalom race—2 out of 41.

And then the breakthrough came. Everything fit together perfectly. Picabo's aggressive attack of the mountain worked. Mistakes and falls disappeared. Old injuries vanished. The reward came. A gold medal replaced years of what-ifs. Picabo Street stood firmly on her mountain atop the 1998 Olympic medal podium.

Sometimes in life nothing seems to go right. Injuries keep us out of athletic competition or lessen our chances of winning. Someone smarter, more skilled, or with better connections earns the place we wanted. We don't win the gold medal or even a silver or bronze. Life isn't always fair, and hard work doesn't always result in success.

But God favors us with His presence. Even when the rest of the world seems to be slipping and sliding, He helps us reach the mountain of His care and stand firmly on the peak of His love.

Search the internet or a sports encyclopedia for specific information about the super giant slalom and other ski races. Picture yourself in the start house high on the mountain preparing for your run. Reread and think about the words of Psalm 30:7.

"Can anyone hide in secret places so that I cannot see him?" declares the Lord. —Jeremiah 23:24

The Boston Marathon has been run every year since 1896. The 1967 race over the 26-mile, 385-yard course drew more than 700 contestants and 200,000 spectators.

A 20-year-old Syracuse University journalism student entered the competition as K. Switzer. The credentials committee processed the application and issued the runner a cardboard placard with the number 261.

The rules required a pre-race physical, but K. Switzer substituted a health certificate supplied by fellow runner Arnold Briggs. Two miles into the running, officials discovered the "K" didn't stand for Kevin, Kenneth, or Karl, but Katherine.

Will Cloney, the Boston Marathon director, ordered the press bus stopped and attempted to remove Ms. Switzer by force. But three collegiate friends, Arnold Briggs, Everett Rice, and Thomas C. Miller, intervened on her behalf. K. Switzer blended into the pack and finished the race unofficially in 4 hours and 20 minutes.

A second female runner entered the Boston Marathon in an unofficial capacity. Roberta Gibb, 23-year-old daughter of a Tufts College chemistry professor, hid near the starting point behind a bush. Just before the gun sounded, she slipped into the pack.

Ms. Gibb ran the entire course except for the final yard. A race official stepped in front of her just prior to her crossing the finish line. Gibb's unofficial clocking would have been 3:27:17.

A five-year battle ensued over women's eligibility in the marathon. In 1972, both sexes earned the privilege of competition. But another twelve years elapsed before the Olympic games recognized the event.

Katherine Switzer attempted to disguise her true identity from Boston Marathon brass. And for a time, she succeeded. Roberta

Gibb simply tried to make herself invisible to the men who sounded the start. And for a while, she achieved her goal too. But the race course proved too open and their female bodies too obvious. Besides, race officials filled the entire course.

Sometimes, like the two racers, we try to hide. Only we try to conceal ourselves from God. We keep Him in the far back parts of our hearts and minds. We don't pray. We skip worship. We work at not thinking about Him. We keep so busy that we believe He can't creep into our lives.

But it's impossible to elude God. We have no secrets from Him. He fills the entire world and knows every single person. He knows us, and what's more, He loves us.

So don't try to hide. He already knows where you are. Instead, show Him who you are. Grow closer to Him. Pray. Worship. Let Him fill your world.

Put yourself in the place of Katherine Switzer and Roberta Gibb. You've trained hard and really want to run the 26-mile race. You know you can finish the Boston Marathon, but the rules won't let you enter. Think of ways you might be able to make yourself invisible to the authorities. Would you be successful? Then think of ways you try to make yourself invisible to God. Do any of them work? Thank God that He is everywhere, even when we don't want Him to be.

GRAF UPSETS HINGIS IN FRENCH OPEN

A fool gives full vent to his anger, but a wise man keeps himself under control....An angry man stirs up dissension, and a hot-tempered one commits many sins.

—PROVERBS 29:11, 22

German superstar Steffi Graf won her first French Open in 1987. At age 17, she became the youngest player to win the prestigious Grand Slam event. Twelve years and numerous injuries later, the former number-one-ranked player faced the current number-one-ranked player, Martina Hingis, in the 1999 finals at Roland Garros.

Spectators strongly favored the 29 year old over the 18 year old. Graf seemed to enjoy the crowd, while Hingis grew frustrated at their partisanship and the close calls that went against her. In the third game of the opening set, she drew an official's warning for breaking her racket by slamming it onto the court.

After claiming the first set 6–4, Martina appeared to have command. But in the third game of set two, her anger created an ugly scene.

The line judge ruled Hingis' forehand return had landed out. The Swiss native charged to Graf's side of the net, pointed to the mark, and protested the call.

The crowd chanted, "Steffi, Steffi," as Martina's tirade continued. The supervisor of officials assessed Hingis a point penalty for her severe breach of tennis etiquette.

Despite her inconsistent play and childlike behavior, Martina led 5–4 in the second set. She only needed to hold her serve to win the match. But Steffi rallied and took the game as Hingis netted a backhand drop shot. The momentum shifted, and the German claimed the set, 7–5.

Graf bolted to a 3–0 lead in the third set. Hingis challenged briefly, winning games four and five, but Steffi twice broke the

Swiss teen's serve to triumph 6–2.

On match point, Martina produced a cascade of boos with an underhand serve. A second one produced more shouts of "Steffi, Steffi."

Following Graf's victory, Hingis briefly shook her opponent's hand as she tearfully exited the court to a chorus of catcalls. Still crying, she needed the presence of her mother-coach to accept the runner-up trophy.

The victory, Steffi's sixth in the French Open, gave her 22 Grand Slam titles, just 2 behind Margaret Court. In the post-match presentation, she announced the trip to Roland Garros would be her last in singles and bade her adoring French fans au revoir.

Hingis partially composed herself as she stood near the champion. Graf assured the teen she would yet have chances to win the French Open, but Martina knew in her heart she should have won this one.

The crowd supported Graf at the beginning of the match, but Hingis' behavior stirred even more opposition. Her anger resulted in unforced errors and lost opportunities. The better tennis player didn't win. The more self-controlled athlete did.

The Bible contains wise words about anger. The emotion strains relationships. It forces mistakes and removes the focus from where it ought to be to the object of the wrath. Throwing a tantrum, seeing red, flying off the handle, or blowing up serves no useful purpose.

Instead God urges self-control. The wise follow His teaching.

Think of a time when your temper got the upper hand. Maybe you argued with an official or tried to get even. Perhaps it wasn't you, but a teammate or a friend who got mad. Did anger help the situation? Did it make things worse? Decide how you or your friend could have reacted differently. Ask God for the wisdom to practice self-control.

LETTERS CHANGE ELLA MAE RILEY'S LIFE

Or do we need, like some people, letters of recommendation to you or from you? You yourselves are our letter, written on our hearts, known and read by everybody. —2 CORINTHIANS 3:1-2

Ella Mae Riley grew up during the Great Depression in a two-room hut in the small town of Ketchum, Oklahoma. Her father died when she was six, and her mother struggled to provide life's necessities for her two sons and two daughters.

With no money for entertainment, Ella Mae and her two brothers stuffed a dishtowel with rags and shot it through a hoop. Eventually "ragball" gave way to basketball when the young woman entered high school.

Under basketball rules at the time, players stayed at their positions—guards on defense, centers at mid-court to jump for the ball after each basket, and forwards on offense. Riley played forward and shot the ball with precision. She specialized in a hook shot, a two-handed set shot, and a one-handed push shot.

In 1937, Ella Mae scored all of Ketchum's 38 points in a game against Cleora. Her coach sent the box score to the internationally syndicated column, "Ripley's Believe It or Not."

Several months later, a report of Riley's feat, along with a drawing, drew mention in hundreds of newspapers. Thus began a chain of events that changed her life forever.

Helen Stephens, an Olympic sprinter from Missouri, offered the small-town girl a spot on her barnstorming basketball team, the Olympic Co-eds. Ella Mae pawned a ring to pay for the bus ticket to join the team in Springfield, Illinois.

Stephens inserted Riley into the starting line-up the moment she arrived. Drawing upon the Oklahoma native's Cherokee heritage and dark hair, the promoter billed her as "Little Chief Riley."

Thousands nationwide witnessed the women's team adorned in red satin uniforms taking on all challengers. Riley starred with her spectacular shooting. In a game against a male team of former all-state Michigan players, she scored 68 points.

Nine months and 26 states later, the barnstorming tour ended. Ella Mae returned to Oklahoma to college. But life on the road had left Riley hungry for adventure. She graduated, took a job with millionaire John Paul Getty's company, and earned her pilot's license.

Ella Mae Riley's entire future changed because of two letters—a letter about her written by her coach to a newspaper column and a letter to her from a former Olympian who read the column and then offered work, travel, and adventure. The teen's life became vastly different from what it might have been because of the written word.

Words provide information, capture emotion, incite action, and alter attitudes. Words change lives. Words written and read at the right time influence history. Words can be powerful tools for good or for evil.

God gave words to the psalmist, the prophets, the gospel-writers, and all those who penned the Holy Spirit's inspiration into the Bible. And throughout the centuries, that book has influenced all those who have read its pages and written its lessons on their hearts.

Think about special letters you have received or written. What kind of influence did they have? Paul wrote letters that changed the world. Most of the New Testament is made up of his letters to the first Christians. Read one today (Philemon is a good one) and thank God for the book He has written you, the Bible.

Emma George Flies in Pole Vault

You said in your heart, "I will ascend about the tops of the clouds; I will make myself like the Most High." But you are brought down to the grave, to the depths of the pit.

—ISAIAH 14:13-14

Emma George began her athletic career as a child trapeze artist in the Flying Fruit Fly circus. Acrobatics eventually led to her running sprints and competing in the long jump in high school.

The arts and commerce major at Deakin University in Melbourne, Australia, noticed the school's pole vaulters practicing and decided to give the sport a try. Coach Mark Stewart welcomed his new protégée enthusiastically. Within two years, Emma had risen to world-class standards.

The European track circuit added the women's pole vault as an event in the early 1990s. The International Amateur Athletic Federation recognized the first world record in May 1992. China's Sun Caiyun set the mark at 13 feet, $3^1/_2$ inches.

Emma rewrote the record book on November 30, 1995, at a meet in Melbourne, Australia. Her leap of 13 feet, $11^1/_4$ eclipsed Caiyun's record of 13 feet $10^1/_2$ set less than a month earlier.

For more than three years, the Australian's name remained at the top of the vaulting list and the height of her record steadily climbed. Others improved their marks, but none bested the former child acrobat.

In February 1999 at the Sydney Grand Prix, Emma easily cleared her opening heights. With the gold medal assured, the 25-year-old vaulter begged her coach for a record attempt.

He agreed, and the judges set the height at 15 feet, 1 inch, a mere 1/4 inch above her best. Emma took a deep breath, bolted down the runway, set her pole, and sailed cleanly over the bar. The record-setting leap marked the sixteenth time the 5-foot-7-

inch vaulter had established a new women's standard.

The year 2000 not only ushered in a new century, it also greeted the summer Olympic games. Sydney, Australia, in George's native country, was named to host the pinnacle of amateur athletics. Those games debuted the women's pole vault as an Olympic sport. The gold medalist automatically captured the Olympic record.

Imagine running 150 feet down the track, planting a long and thin fiberglass pole into the ground, soaring over the delicately held crossbar, and finally falling into a pit filled with soft, cushiony material. Pole vaulting takes an athlete quickly from ground level to between two and three times her height, to below the ground; all in a matter of seconds.

God has a way of doing the same to pride and ego. We like to feel important and in charge. We sometimes soar to such heights that we try to take control of our lives instead of leaving them in God's hands. We want to make ourselves like the Almighty.

But no matter how many people look up to us, no matter how many medals we take or how much money we make, God is God. And eventually, He will bring us back down to earth.

Think of some famous people who moved from great popularity and prominence to facing their failings. One example is the United States President who resigned his office. Compare your list with a friend's. Ask God to help you keep your pride and ego in check and to create a humble spirit in your life.

In fact, the law requires that nearly everything be cleansed with blood, and without the shedding of blood there is no forgiveness. —HEBREWS 9:22

Kelli Kuehne struggled in 1998, her first year on the Ladies Professional Golf Association tour. She missed the cut in her first seven tournaments and finished the year ranked 124th in total winnings.

Following her disappointing rookie season, the two-time United States Women's Amateur Champion searched for the source of her difficulties. Once she pinpointed it, Kelli developed a four-step approach toward elimination.

She gained needed strength through improved workouts and diet. Kuehne's short-game coach, Tracy Phillips, became her full-time caddy. And she scheduled extra practice with her swing coach, Hank Haney.

But the diabetic and former University of Texas golfer obtained her biggest edge with a new insulin pump. The device allowed her to play without taking shots and only required pricking a finger to test her blood-sugar level.

Kelli entered the final round of the 1999 Corning Classic trailing the leader, two-time tournament champion Rosie Jones, by a single stroke. On day four, the second-year pro performed with the poise of a veteran and the enthusiasm of a rookie.

Kuehne flawlessly played the front nine. Aided by an eagle on the par-5 number 5 hole, she carded a 31 and moved into a 5-stroke lead.

Kelli checked her blood-sugar level on the 13th tee box. It registered a 67, far below a normal reading of 120, but the Dallas native decided to try to finish the round.

Following a 12-foot birdie putt on number 14, Kuehne headed toward the clubhouse with a 6-stroke margin. But stress and weakness due to low blood sugar began to exact their toll.

The 22 year old double bogeyed 15, parred 16, and bogeyed 17 and 18. Meanwhile Jones finished in a flurry on the final four holes, making a birdie on 16 and parring the rest.

But Kelli Kuehne survived the onslaught and took her first professional championship by one stroke, 278–279.

The golfer had confronted her obstacles head-on and learned the secrets of a champion. Face individual challenges. Don't give in to problems. Work hard. Sacrifice. Stay on top of the situation.

Most athletes never give much thought to their blood sugar. Oh, they might feel a little tired and decide to drink a sports drink or eat an energy bar for a boost. Not Kuehne. Blood stays in her thoughts all day every day. Her diabetes requires constant monitoring. Low readings and tiredness can turn into a hypoglycemic reaction, and could even be a life-threatening problem. Insulin keeps her body stable, but without it, her own blood could kill her or save her life.

In the same way, blood is important to every Christian. Old Testament law required blood sacrifices to cleanse for sin. It was the only way to earn God's forgiveness.

Jesus changed that. He gave Himself for all the wrongs of all the people of all time. His blood became the sacrifice for us. He simply asks that we earnestly seek His forgiveness and trust in Him. Christ has given us His saving blood.

Learn all you can about diabetics and their disease. Note the following symptoms:

    Extreme thirst

    Blurry vision from time to time

    Frequent urination

    Unusual tiredness or drowsiness

    Unexplained weight loss

Ask God to give strength to all those who suffer from diabetes. Thank God for the gift of Jesus and His sacrifice.

ALABAMA-UCLA GAME ENDS ON ERROR

If it is true that I have gone astray, my error remains my concern alone. —JOB 19:4

The NCAA basketball tournament has witnessed last-minute heroics and controversial finishes. In the second round of the 1998 Midwest Regional, the University of Alabama Crimson Tide and the University of California at Los Angeles Lady Bruins provided both.

With the teams knotted at 73–73, UCLA took over the ball with 23 seconds remaining following an Alabama turnover. Seconds clicked down, and the contest appeared headed for overtime.

But Tausha Mills fouled the Lady Bruin's Maylana Martin. Mills connected on one of two free throws to put UCLA ahead, 74–73.

Following a time-out, Alabama's Brittney Ezell inbounded the ball with 0.8 seconds to play. Her court-length pass hit Dominique Canty who tipped it to Latoya Caudle.

As the buzzer sounded, Caudle fired a jumper from the top of the key. The ball swished through the net. Alabama wildly celebrated its 75–74 triumph.

But Lady Bruin coach Kathy Olivier dashed madly toward the officials. She claimed the clock started late and that time should have expired before Caudle's shot. Olivier also complained that Ezell illegally ran the baseline before making her long inbound pass. Players may move laterally following a shot, but not after a time-out.

The referees huddled for more than 20 minutes watching a videotape replay. Television cameras indicated Ezell indeed ran the baseline illegally. However, the officials denied Olivier's protest and allowed the play to stand. They justified their error by stating the violation must be called immediately and cannot be reversed by viewing a taped replay.

The Lady Crimson Tide reigned victorious.

Should Olivier's complaint have been upheld? Maybe or maybe not. Should UCLA have won? Maybe or maybe not. Was the decision right? Maybe or maybe not. Was the decision fair? Maybe or maybe not.

But regardless of what was right or fair, the referees had the responsibility and the power to make the decision. Although the outcome of the game impacted two schools, the initial error and whether to correct it became the officials' concern. It was theirs alone.

In the Bible, Job found himself saying something similar. Bildad, Eliphaz, and Zophar attacked their friend Job with words. They delighted in pointing out what they saw as his errors. They tried to justify themselves by tearing him down. When Job had finally had enough, he let them know any mistake he had made was his concern alone.

Too often in athletics and in life we play the blame game. We seem more interested in correcting the mistakes others make than in handling our own. We find it easier to blame teammates or officials or equipment or the weather for our defeats. We overlook calls that went our way early in the contest to focus on questionable decisions officials made near the end.

But God wants us to take responsibility for our own actions and errors.

Think about the last time you blamed a mistake or a loss on the officials, a teammate, or someone or something else. Honestly examine your actions. Ask yourself if you enjoy pointing out people's errors in order to make yourself look better. Pray that God will help you take ownership of your own faults and let others be concerned about theirs.

WITTY WINS TREASURED MEDALS

Do not store up for yourselves treasures on earth, where moth and rust destroy, and where thieves break in and steal. But store up for yourselves treasures in heaven, where moth and rust do not destroy, and where thieves do not break in and steal. For where your treasure is, there your heart will be also. —MATTHEW 6:19-21

Chris Witty grew up in West Allis, Wisconsin, a blue-collar section of Milwaukee. She began skating at age 12, using a pair of rusted, oversized skates because her father, a welder, lost his job when the Allis Chalmers plant closed.

The family scrimped and saved to afford lessons. Chris' mother struggled to feed and clothe a husband and four children from her salary at an insurance company. Chris and her brother, Mike, took paper routes to earn money for equipment and travel.

Economic hardship almost forced Chris from the rink, but the public took notice of the rising star. An anonymous California benefactor sent the young girl her first pair of new skates.

Witty's hard work and perseverance reaped rewards. At age 18 she earned a spot on the 1994 U.S. Olympic speedskating team and placed 23rd at the Lillehammer (Norway) Games.

The skater continued to improve. In 1997, she set a world record in the 1,000 meters and an American record in the 1,500 meters. Medal hopes abounded for the 22-year-old Wisconsin native when she qualified for the 1998 United States Olympic squad.

Experts, however, expected little from the Americans in Nagano, Japan. The country's speedskating superstar Bonnie Blair, a five-time Olympic gold medalist, had retired from the ice.

Witty surprised everyone with a third place finish in the 1,500 meters. Her time of 1:58.97 bettered the American record she had set the previous October by almost a second. Marianne Timmer of the Netherlands turned in a world record performance of 1:57.58 to claim the gold.

Two days later, Chris raced her strongest event, the 1,000 meters. Fueled by her unexpected 1,500 meter success, Witty's odds of obtaining gold appeared good.

But her Dutch opponent rose to the forefront once more. Timmer set an Olympic record of 1:16.51, and the American took silver.

When it came to silver and gold, Chris' family had very little. Money became very scarce in the eight years Walter Witty couldn't find steady work. Diane's salary and the children's part-time jobs stretched to the limit.

But the family had treasures far beyond earthly goods. They loved and supported each other. They developed persistence, determination, and heart. And they had friends, even some they never met. When her family couldn't provide, friends did.

In 1998, Chris Witty's heavenly treasures turned into earthly ones. Shortly before the Olympics, her father found a permanent job. Diane and Walter traveled to Japan to watch their daughter earn bronze and silver.

In His Sermon on the Mount, Jesus urges us to pay more attention to building heart treasures than material ones. Money and possessions last only a little while. They can be stolen or destroyed. And even when such riches remain, death takes them away.

Instead, Jesus says, we should acquire heavenly treasures. They last forever.

Make a list of your five most prized material posses-sions. Estimate how long they will last. List five spiritual quali-ties that will last forever. Ask God to help you store treasures in heaven.

BLANKERS-KOEN HOPES FOR FOUR GOLDS

But if we hope for what we do not yet have, we wait for it patiently. —ROMANS 8:24-25

Francina "Fanny" Koen made the 1936 Dutch Olympic team at age 18. She placed sixth in the high jump and fifth as a member of the 4 x 100 relay. The Netherlands native considered the highlight of her competition the acquisition of Jesse Owens' autograph.

Fanny hoped for future Olympic endeavors, but World War II forced cancellation of the 1940 and 1944 games. By 1948, she had married her coach, Jan Blankers, and borne two children.

The Dutch athlete also held world records in the 100-meter dash, 80-meter hurdles, high jump, long jump, and two relays. But most considered the 30 year old past her athletic prime.

Blankers-Koen worked out diligently, pushing her baby carriage to Amsterdam Stadium each day. She quieted her critics at the 1948 Olympics, winning the 100 meters in 11.9 seconds with a 3-meter margin of victory.

In her next event, the 80-meter hurdles, Fanny struggled against English runner Maureen Gardner. As they awaited the results, the band played "God Save the King," and the Dutch runner assumed she had lost. But the song honored the entrance of the British royal family, and the photo finish revealed Blankers-Koen as the victor.

The pressure to capture a third gold medal brought Fanny to the brink of a mental breakdown. Her husband attempted to calm her fears, but his words of encouragement evoked tears. The 30-year-old Olympian eventually overcame her fright and won the race by 7 meters, the largest winning margin in women's 200-meter history.

In her final event, the 4 x 100 relay, Blankers-Koen took the baton on the anchor leg in fourth place. She closed the gap and nipped Australia's Joyce King at the finish. Fanny became the only woman to win four track and field gold medals in a single Olympics.

The Dutch runner dared to hope she could win an Olympic medal. Fanny didn't possess the wishful kind of hope that says, "Wouldn't it be nice if. . . ." Instead, she held the hope that knows there's a strong possibility if backed by planning, patience, practice, and perseverance.

Blankers-Koen waited, and while she waited, she worked. She planned how she would train and take care of her two little ones. She patiently persevered through the war years, believing that the end of World War II would bring a new beginning to the Olympics. The young mother practiced and practiced and practiced still more.

At last Francina Blankers-Koen stood atop the medal stand four times as her nation's anthem played four times. Fanny's hope had become real.

But in life, there's another kind of hope. It's a hope that's real and certain from the beginning. It's the hope we have through faith in Jesus Christ—the hope of heaven. Spending eternity with God isn't wishful thinking. It isn't even Fanny's kind of hope backed by patience and hard work. Instead, it's a certain hope for the future. If we trust Jesus Christ as our Savior, we will live forever with Him. Hallelujah!

Look up the word "hope" in an unabridged dictionary. Read all the different meanings. Praise God for the definition that assures eternity with Him.

UNC CHALLENGES CONFIDENT TENNESSEE

This is the confidence we have in approaching God: that if we ask anything according to His will, He hears us. And if we know that He hears us—whatever we ask—we know that we have what we asked of Him.

—1 JOHN 5:14-15

Many believe the 1998 University of Tennessee's women's basketball team was the greatest of all time. Seldom did the Lady Volunteers face a serious challenge. They defeated every opponent and averaged a winning margin of 30 points in every victory.

But in the NCAA Midwest Regional finals, the Lady Tar Heels of the University of North Carolina (UNC) refused to be intimidated.

North Carolina trailed at halftime, 33–27, but sprinted to a 40–37 lead by breaking Tennessee's trapping defense. The Lady Tar Heels attacked the backcourt with quick, over-the-top passes and found easy layups on the other end.

On defense, the underdogs kept National Player-of-the-Year, Chamique Holdsclaw, in check with taller inside players. During one 22-minute stretch, the All-American forward scored only 2 points.

Chamique seemed to panic, throwing up hurried, awkward shots. She even tossed an air ball from underneath her basket and appeared to have lost her confidence.

Sensing an upset, North Carolina's Tracy Reid sprinted for layup after layup. Jessica Gaspar hit a jumper to put the Tar Heels in front, 61–49, with 7:34 left to play. The Lady Volunteers had never trailed by a margin that large all season.

But Holdsclaw fueled a furious comeback. Her defense, rebounding, and free throw accuracy led a 15–1 Tennessee run in less than 3 minutes.

Chamique tied the score at 62–all following a steal by Tamika

Catchings. Moments later, she intercepted a pass and hit a short jumper to put the Lady Vols in front, 64–62.

The Lady Tar Heels rallied, however, as Holdsclaw drew her fourth foul. UNC edged ahead, 67–66.

Tennessee refused to falter and confidently sank free throws. Chamique hit 2 to regain the lead for the Lady Vols. Teresa Geter made a follow shot, and Holdsclaw canned another pair for a 72–67 margin.

Chanel Wright nailed a 3-pointer, but the Lady Tar Heels could draw no closer. Kellie Jolly's 2 free throws swished the net with 19.9 seconds remaining, and Chamique hit the final 2 as the clock ticked down to single digits. Tennessee prevailed 76–70 for their 37th victory of the season.

What accounted for the victory? What made the difference? Both teams possessed talent. Both teams enjoyed outstanding coaching. Both schools owned winning traditions. In the end, confidence created the edge.

God provides confidence in life. We can be sure of Him and His love. Our Heavenly Father provides certainty in a world of uncertainty. He promises that He hears and answers our prayers if we pray according to His will.

God also provides confidence in death. If we trust in Jesus Christ for salvation, we will spend eternity with Him. In the end, confidence makes the difference.

The dictionary defines confidence as self-assurance, faith, a feeling of trust or certainty. Practice a skill or task until you feel confident in your ability. It can be anything from shooting free throws to baking chocolate chip cookies to sharing your faith. Ask God to give you the confidence to do your best for Him. Thank Him for the confidence He gives both now and forever.

First Woman Swims English Channel

And God said, "Let the water under the sky be gathered to one place, and let dry ground appear." And it was so. God called the dry ground "land," and the gathered waters he called "seas." And God saw that it was good.

—GENESIS 1:9-10

The morning of August 6, 1926 dawned cold and damp on the shores of northwestern France. Gertrude "Trudy" Ederle covered her body with six pounds of thick black grease and waded into the chilling waters of the English Channel off Cape Gris-Nez. At eight minutes past seven, the 19-year-old swimmer began her journey toward the English shore.

Only five people—all men—had completed the 20-mile journey prior to Ederle's attempt. A native of Argentina, Enrique Tiraboschi, held the fastest time at slightly more than $16^1/_2$ hours.

A French tugboat, the *Alsace*, chugged along next to the American swimmer. It carried her trainer Thomas Burgess, her father Henry, her sister Margaret, and three fellow swimmers: Louis Timson, Ishak Helmy, and Lillian Cameron. A sign with an arrow reading, "This Way Ole Kid," pointed toward the British shore and offered encouragement.

The first leg of the watery journey unfolded smoothly. Ederle covered four miles in about three hours. Trudy drank some beef broth and hot chocolate to maintain her strength.

About 1:30 in the afternoon, the weather turned nasty. Drenching rain poured from the sky, strong winds blew, and the temperature dropped rapidly.

The boat crew sang such popular songs as "Yes, We Have No Bananas" and "Let Me Call You Sweetheart" to boost Trudy's spirits. The waves became stronger, but the American swimmer refused to quit.

Darkness settled in, and lanterns dotted the English country-

side. Hundreds scanned the shoreline, peering into the inky blackness for the young woman.

At 9:39 P.M., Gertrude Ederle emerged from the water at Kingsdown, England. She had completed the perilous swim in a record-breaking time of 14 hours and 31 minutes.

When Trudy returned to the United States, she rode down Broadway in an open limousine with New York Mayor Jimmy Walker. Ticker tape rained from the skies, turning the blacktop into a blanket of white.

The following September, the *Saturday Evening Post* wrote, "In all the annals of sport there is no finer record than that rung up by this young American girl."

Many people go to the sea for rest and relaxation. The sound of the waves, the coolness of the water, and the sparkle of sunlight diamonds on the surf offer a feeling of calm. Jesus often renewed His spirit by taking time alone or with His twelve disciples at the Sea of Galilee.

Others view the water as a source of food or income. The smell of fish cooking over a campfire and anticipating its freshly caught flavor offers a different feeling about the sea. Fishermen brothers Simon Peter and Andrew and James and John left their nets to follow Jesus and became His disciples.

For a few, like Trudy Ederle, the sea becomes a challenge. They swim, sail, surf, or scuba. They push their bodies to enter iron-man or woman competitions, to sail in regattas, or to swim the English Channel. Jesus challenged the sea Himself as He walked on its surface.

But however we see the sea, it is God's creation. We, like Him, must pronounce it, "Good."

Visit a river, lake, or beach. Enjoy listening to the water and feeling its coolness. If you can't go to the shore put on a CD of ocean sounds or simply imagine them. Think of how these sounds were important in Jesus' life and praise God for His creation.

Calmness can lay great errors to rest.

—ECCLESIASTES 10:4

The United States Women's national team placed a 42-game winning streak on the line when they faced Australia in the semifinals of the 1998 International Softball Federation World Championship. The Americans took a 1–0 lead in the sixth inning when Shelly Stokes doubled, Amy Chellevold singled, and Lisa Fernandez grounded out to drive in Stokes.

The Australians immediately countered. Fiona Hanes singled, and Simmone Morrow reached on an error. The coach moved Fernandez from third base to pitcher. She gave up a hit to Peta Ederbone, allowing Hanes to tie the game.

With the contest knotted 1–1 after the regulation nine innings, international tie-breaker rules came into play. The final batter of the previous inning began the subsequent inning on second as a baserunner.

Neither team pushed a run across in the tenth or eleventh. In the bottom of the twelfth, Australia's Ederbone hit with Morrow at second. Following a fielder's choice, Fernandez's throwing error allowed Morrow to score. The American's string of victories ended.

But hope remained for the United States. An elimination game against China the following afternoon would determine who faced Australia in the nightcap for the world title.

Lisa Fernandez took the mound and pitched almost flawlessly. She allowed only 5 hits while striking out 7. Sheila Douty staked the Americans to a 2–0 lead with a first-inning home run, and the U.S. won easily, 4–0.

The four-time University of California at Los Angeles All-American pitcher also drew the starting assignment against the Aussies. She aided her cause with a towering solo homer in the first inning. Then, torrential rains descended. The downpour delayed the contest for six hours. Play resumed half an hour past midnight.

The interruption never fazed Fernandez as she dominated the powerful Australian hitters, giving up only 1 hit and whiffing 14 batters. The 1–0 lead held as the Americans claimed their fourth consecutive world championship and earned the number one seed at the 2000 Olympics.

Imagine blowing a 42-game winning streak with a throwing error. How devastating! Lisa Fernandez must have felt just awful. She surely had a sleepless night imagining what could have been.

But she composed herself. A victory against China became more important than the loss to Australia. With a sense of calm, she pitched a winner and put her error to rest.

When the Americans found themselves playing Australia again for the world championship, they felt butterflies in their stomachs and knots in their chests. In spite of the unnerving rain delay, Lisa stayed composed. She walked off the field a winner, both at the plate and on the mound.

We all make mistakes. But God says it's how we deal with our blunders that's important. Calmness helps minimize the results of our errors. By remaining levelheaded and self-controlled, we can usually put our mistakes behind us.

Watch a softball or baseball game, or look at the box scores on the sports page of a newspaper. Note the number of errors each team made. Did the team that won make fewer? Or were they able to remain calm and compensate? Ask God to help you remain composed when you make a mistake.

Remember those earlier days after you had received the light, when you stood your ground in a great contest in the face of suffering. —HEBREWS 10:32

Deborah Compagnoni's injured knees make it impossible for her to lift heavy weights or to conduct a standard conditioning regime. But in the 1998 Winter Olympics, the Italian skier accomplished a feat no other has matched.

At age 20, Compagnoni captured her first Olympic gold medal in the 1992 Albertville (France) super-G, winning in a time of 1:21.22. Two years later in the Lillehammer (Norway) games, she took first place with a 2:30.97 in her trademark event, the giant slalom.

In between competitions, the dark-haired skier spent more time in hospitals than on the slopes. She underwent four knee operations and another to remove an intestinal blockage. In addition, Deborah suffered through a serious kidney infection.

During her first eight World Cup seasons, Deborah competed in only 40 races. Most skiers enter that number in a single year.

Despite her physical limitations, the popular Italian prepared to defend her title at the 1998 Nagano (Japan) games. Heavy sleet falling on Mount Higashidate made both visibility and maneuvering difficult.

But Compagnoni remained calm. While other skiers struggled to find their edges and establish a rhythm, the charismatic athlete maintained her speed and fluidity.

After the first run, she led France's Sophie LeFranc by almost a full second. Her chief competitors, German's Hilde Gerg and Martina Ertl, trailed farther behind as they battled the slope's treacherous conditions.

When Deborah readied for her second run, she needed only a

respectable time to capture first place. But the two-time Olympic gold medalist turned in a stunning performance.

She completed the course in a winning time of 2:50.59. Austria's Alexandra Meissnitzer claimed the silver, and Germany's Katja Seizinger took the bronze. Compagnoni's 1.81 margin of victory represented the largest in Olympic giant slalom history since Canada's Nancy Greene won by 2.64 seconds in 1968.

The 27 year old's giant slalom victory made her the first skier, male or female, to capture Alpine golds in three Olympics.

Not once, not twice, but three times Deborah Compagnoni topped the Olympic medal stand. In not one, not two, but in three different countries in three different years, she felt the pride of hearing her national anthem played.

Deborah's extraordinary feat became even more extraordinary in the face of her injuries. Unable to use normal training methods, she improvised, and she suffered. The Italian woman did the best she could to get ready for the games held once every four years. She hoped her best would be good enough, and it was.

Life includes suffering. God never promised that His followers would be exempt from illness, injuries, or hard times. Our Heavenly Father commends us when we overcome obstacles to stand firm in Him. And He promises that He will be near us, support us, guide us, and love us through our difficult days.

Pray for someone you know who is ill, injured, or suffering through hard times. Write a short note or call to let the person know of your prayers and to offer encouragement during difficult days.

Mighty Macs Play Immaculate Basketball

For as the soil makes the sprout come up and a garden causes seeds to grow, so the Sovereign Lord will make righteousness and praise spring up before all nations.

—ISAIAH 61:11

Collegiate women's basketball originated in humble circumstances. In the game's infancy, teams played at odd times in dimly lighted gyms with mere handfuls of spectators in attendance.

But as the sport progressed and players improved, fans took notice. Immaculata, a women's college of about 500 students near Philadelphia, developed into an early powerhouse.

In the early 1970s, Coach Cathy Rush took the Mighty Macs to the AIAW title games five times in six years and captured three consecutive AIAW national championships. The NCAA didn't sanction women's basketball at that time.

At one point, the team won 35 straight games before losing to Queens College of New York in 1974. The following January, Immaculata became one of the first two women's teams to appear on national television, defeating the University of Maryland, 85–63. In February, promoters staged a rematch between Queens and Immaculata at New York's Madison Square Garden. The women's contest preceded a men's game between Fairfield and the University of Massachusetts.

Much to everyone's surprise, 11,969 fans flocked to the arena. Banners, pompoms, mascots, and a 500-member Mighty Mac student cheering section engulfed the famous sporting site.

Amazingly, the vast majority of basketball fans bought tickets to watch the women and not their male counterparts. A Garden employee estimated only about 4,000 remained by halftime of the second contest.

Immaculata and Queens provided their partisans with a performance that matched the pre-game hype. The Mighty Macs avenged their previous loss with a 65–61 victory. Sophomore guard Mary Schraff paced Immaculata with 12 points and 9 rebounds.

To speed up the game, officials adopted a 30-second shot clock for women's basketball. Fans responded favorably to the fast pace and constant action. Many predicted, and rightly so, the men's game would eventually incorporate a similar rule.

Coaches, players, and fans alike praised both teams and the opportunity given to showcase their abilities. After viewing the contest, most skeptics admitted the women hustled and performed as skillfully as the men.

The Mighty Mac women were talented. Mary Schraff, the 1975 Madison Square Garden top-scorer, began coaching at her alma mater in 1985. Other Immaculata stand-outs, Theresa Shank Grentz, Rene Muth Portland, and Marianne Crawford Stanley, coach women's basketball teams at the University of Illinois, Penn State, and the University of California, Berkeley respectively. Grentz also led the 1992 Olympic Women's Basketball Team.

The soil was ready and the garden ripe for women's basketball to sprout and grow at Immaculata. Eventually, the seeds spread through United States colleges and universities and into the Olympic games.

God also spreads seeds throughout the world. They are the seeds of His love and righteousness. Praise and dedication to the Sovereign Lord sprout from those kernels as His name spreads to all nations and all peoples.

Look at seed packets in a garden center or grocery store. Consider selecting some to grow herbs, flowers, or vegetables. Read the information about light, temperature, and soil conditions required before making a choice. Think of some ways you can sow the seeds of God's Word in other people's lives. Praise God that the seeds of His righteousness can grow in any conditions or circumstances.

> *But I, with a song of thanksgiving, will sacrifice to you.* —JONAH 2:9

Brandi Chastain emerged as an American soccer superstar. After leading San Jose's Archbishop Mitty High School to three California state championships, she entered the University of California at Berkeley.

Soccer American named her Freshman of the Year in 1986, but ligament surgery sidelined the young woman in 1987 and 1988. Following her rehabilitation, Brandi transferred to Santa Clara University.

The Broncos made back-to-back NCAA Final Four appearances during Chastain's junior and senior seasons. She joined the U.S. Women's National Team as a back-up forward and participated on the first FIFA Women's World Cup squad in 1991.

The Californian eventually left America to play professionally in Japan. Her team, Skiroki Serena, named Chastain their Most Valuable Player, and the league selected her as the only foreigner among its top eleven players.

After a two-year layoff, Brandi missed playing for her own country. But younger players such as Mia Hamm, Kristine Lilly, Tiffeny Milbrett, and Shannon MacMillan had risen to star status.

Realizing her limitations, the All-American switched positions from striker to the less glamorous role of defender. But the transition earned Chastain a starting spot on both the 1996 Olympic and 1998 Goodwill Games gold medal teams.

In the 1998 U.S. Women's Cup tournament, the field included Mexico, Russia, Brazil, and the United States. The Americans routed Mexico, 9–0, in the opener. The second match against Russia proved more difficult, but again the U.S. prevailed, 4–0.

In the final match, Brazil took advantage of forward and midfielder speed, forcing the Americans to play at the Brazilian pace.

The game remained scoreless until late in the first half.

Following a corner kick in the 32nd minute, Chastain headed the ball across the goalmouth. Joy Fawcett, the tournament's MVP, shot it past Brazilian goalkeeper Maravilha for the first score.

Eleven minutes later, midfielder Michelle Akers scored her 98th international goal from 7 yards out, swatting Mia Hamm's free kick into the net. Late in the second half, the Americans collected a final point when Chastain passed to Debbie Keller off a free kick.

The 3–0 triumph avenged a previous 1–0 loss to Brazil. The victory also assured the United States a berth in the 1999 World Cup tournament. And in her new position, Brandi Chastain had assisted on 2 of her country's 3 goals.

Brandi had a decision to make. Did she want to continue to try to score goals, compete to be a star, and maybe not be named to the United States soccer team? Or was she willing to move to a less visible position, stay in the background, and likely make the team? She chose the latter, sacrificing personal ego to play. And what's more, she did so with a positive attitude and thanksgiving in her heart.

In the Bible, Jonah had a decision to make. God asked him to sacrifice his ego to preach in the wicked city, Nineveh. The prophet boarded a ship going the other direction. When the sailors discovered Jonah's disobedience had caused a dangerous storm, they threw him overboard.

During the three days and three nights Jonah lived inside a great fish, he changed his attitude. Not only did he choose to sacrifice and preach to Nineveh, he decided to go with thanksgiving.

Read the short Book of Jonah in your Bible. It's less than three pages. Remember, resentful sacrifice doesn't accomplish God's purpose. Joyful sacrifice does, so ask God to help you sacrifice with thanksgiving.

FIRST BLACK FEMALE WINS GOLD

> *When I called him he was but one, and I blessed him and made him many.* —ISAIAH 51:2

Circumstances beyond her control prevented Alice Coachman from winning a multitude of Olympic medals. World War II canceled the 1940 and 1944 games while the young woman represented Alabama's Tuskegee Institute.

The Albany, Georgia native dominated the high jump and sprints for almost a decade. She won the Amateur Athletic Union high jump competition every year from 1939 to 1948. During the same time period, the black athlete also captured five 50-meter firsts and three in the 100-meter event.

Her Olympic opportunity finally arrived in 1948. Coachman and ten others comprised the United States women's track squad.

The team traveled to London on board the *SS America*. The ship's rich food and luxurious facilities tempted many to overeat and overindulge.

The effects of the long voyage and lack of proper training soon became evident. One by one the talented American female athletes lost. Until the games' final day, the United States women's team had captured only one single bronze medal. Audrey Patterson claimed third in the 200 meters.

Even that award carried taint. In 1975, a rediscovered photo of the finish revealed Australia's Shirley Strickland clearly placed third, and Patterson took fourth.

The high jump occurred on the final day. At 5 feet, 3 inches, the field narrowed to three competitors: Coachman, France's Micheline Ostermeyer, and Great Britain's Dorothy Tyler.

Ostermeyer went out quickly, and only Coachman and Tyler remained. At the 5'6" mark, the American cleared on her first attempt while Tyler missed. The British contestant achieved the height on her second try, but neither could jump higher.

Coachman claimed first on the basis of fewer misses and became America's first black female Olympic gold medalist.

Albany honored its Olympic heroine with a motorcade and a ceremony at the Municipal Auditorium. But the specter of segregation loomed over the celebration.

The crowd was forced to sit in two sections—black and white. The platform participants divided into two groups—black and white. The white male mayor droned on about Georgia's 1936 white Olympic medalist, Forrest Towns, and never looked at Coachman as she sat in silence.

But Alice was the honoree, the first black woman Olympic gold medalist and the only "real" female track and field medalist in the 1948 games. How tragic that the prejudice of the mayor and many others in Albany took away from Alice Coachman's great moment. What should have been a time of coming together to share an accomplishment became an instant of separation.

Since 1948, many have followed the one as black female athletes regularly earn Olympic medals. And hopefully, today's celebrations feature integration and inclusion as all races and both genders show pride in American victories.

God wants it that way. He created all human beings equally and in His image.

Ask yourself these questions: Do you feel most comfortable around people who look like you in race, nationality, age, education, language, and income? Do disabled people make you feel uncomfortable? Does your church contain different types of persons or are they mostly the same? How would you describe your neighborhood? Do you live a cookie-cutter life with friends just like you? Praise God for His creation of all people of all ages and races. Ask Him to help you expand your world.

Or suppose a woman has ten silver coins and loses one. Does she not light a lamp, sweep the house and search carefully until she finds it? —LUKE 15:8

The International Olympic Committee added curling as a medal sport in 1998 after four appearances in the demonstration category. For four young Canadian women, the decision represented a dream come true.

Curling involves sliding 19.3 kilogram stones with a handle attached along a 146-foot sheet of ice. The scoring resembles horseshoes or shuffleboard. Teams receive a point for each stone closer to the center of the house than their opponent's. The house is a 12-foot circle at the far end of the ice.

The four members of the team each throw two stones. When all 16 stones have been delivered, an inning ends. Games normally consist of 8, 10, or 12 innings.

During play, one team member called the skip moves to the opposite end of the ice. After the thrower curls the stone, the skip gauges its speed. The remaining two players move in front of the stone carrying brooms. The skip commands them to sweep the ice if the stone requires additional speed.

The four Canadian team members, Jan Betker, Marcia Gudereit, Joan McCusker, and Sandra Schmirler, had spent seven years practicing together. They juggled jobs and family along the way. In the 20 months prior to the Nagano games, each took time off to deliver a baby.

Members of the Caledonian Curling Club of Regina, Saskatchewan, the foursome won three world championships prior to their 1998 Olympic performance. During their 1997 title run, Schmirler played despite being six months pregnant.

Though favored, the Canadians narrowly survived in the semifinals, beating Great Britain, 6–5, in extra innings. In the finals against Denmark, they jumped to a 3–0 lead in the first and extended the margin to 6–2 in the sixth. The Danes closed, but Schmirler and her teammates held on for a 7–5 victory and the gold medal.

When the last stone had been thrown and the ice swept for the final time, the Canadian women sprinted to the far end of the rink. Four husbands spilled from the stands, and all eight cried for joy in one embrace.

Who would have ever imagined winning Olympic gold for throwing stones and using brooms? Actually curling dates to early sixteenth-century Scotland. Sweeping remains one of the most unique parts of the event. Partners sweep for each other, removing stray ice particles or snowflakes and smoothing the ice surface. The stronger the power and better the sweep, the farther the stone glides and the greater the chance of winning.

In one of His parables, Jesus also mentions sweeping. As in the Canadian victory, a woman sweeps, and the broom searches for strays, but instead of ice chips, it's for lost coins. And just as in the Olympic medal win, there is great rejoicing.

In the Bible story, a woman loses one of ten silver coins. She lights a lamp and sweeps until she finds it. When she does, she calls her friends and neighbors to rejoice.

Jesus says, "In the same way, I tell you, there is rejoicing in the presence of the angels of God over one sinner who repents."

Just imagine, the angels rejoice more over the salvation of one person than crowds celebrate over Olympic gold.

Read about curling in an encyclopedia or on the internet. Try the sport if there's ice available. Praise God for His concern for every single person, including you!

He heals the brokenhearted and binds up their wounds. —PSALM 147:3

Cheryl Bridges began running at age 16 to lose weight and improve her physique. The administrators at North Central High School in Indianapolis insisted she train on the opposite side of the track to avoid disrupting her male counterparts.

Incredibly, Cheryl developed so quickly as a distance runner she was able to compete in the national cross country championship as a senior. Following graduation, Indiana State offered Bridges an athletic scholarship and made her the first woman to receive the honor at a public university.

In college, the physical education major finished fourth in the World Cross Country Championship. After completing her bachelor's degree in three years, she taught school for a year before moving to California to pursue a master's degree.

Cheryl entered the 1970 Culver City marathon as a training run. At the 20-mile mark, she could run no longer and walked the remaining 6 miles.

The embarrassment spurred her to work on longer distances. The following year, Bridges re-entered the race determined to finish. Not only did she complete the course, Cheryl also ran it in record time. Her clocking of 2:49:40 set a new women's world standard.

Bridges continued to race throughout the 1970s. She cracked the top ten in the national cross country championship ten times between 1965 and 1977.

But in November 1986, tragedy struck. A ventricular tachycardia sent her heart rate soaring to 275 beats per minute for two hours. Running probably saved her life since only a strong heart could have survived the severe fibrillation.

For more than seven years, Cheryl lived a nightmare. Drugs meant to regulate her heart altered her brain. She experienced blurred vision, loss of memory, and lack of strength.

In March 1994, Bridges underwent radio frequency ablation. The seven-hour procedure microwaved the rebel heart cells causing her arrhythmia.

The operation succeeded, and Cheryl celebrated the following day by running 4 miles. Several weeks later she completed a 5K race in less than 7 minutes.

Cheryl Bridges became brokenhearted when her heart began to cause her problems. Not only could she not participate in the sport that had paid for her college education, she couldn't function normally or teach effectively.

And yet that heart that had sustained her running was sustained by her running. Without the years of training and competition, the athlete would probably have died. And who would have ever thought that microwaves could heal her wound. Amazing.

In life, hearts break. Sometimes it's because of physical illness or disease. At other times, the break occurs because of loss—loss of life, loss of friendship, loss of job, loss of home, loss of possessions, or even loss of dreams.

But the psalmist promises that God mends broken hearts and bandages wounded souls if we put ourselves in His hands.

Look around your house for a broken dish or a repair that needs to be made. It could be a plate that cracked and came apart in the dishwasher. Or it could be a chair leg that always comes loose. Using strong glue and patience, put the parts back together. If you've done a good job, the lines where the pieces fit are nearly invisible. Thank God for His ability to perfectly heal broken hearts

Inkster Loves Open Win

I know your deeds, your hard work and your perseverance. . . . Yet I hold this against you: You have forsaken your first love. —REVELATION 2:2, 4

Juli Inkster almost quit the Ladies Professional Golf Association tour. Her once promising career had been side-tracked by inconsistent play, the birth of two daughters, and a heartbreaking playoff loss. But in the 1999 United States Open, the 38 year old achieved triumph after years of frustration.

Inkster took the lead on day two, posting totals of 65 and 69. After her third round of 67, she entered the final day with a 4-stroke margin over Kelli Kuehne and Lorie Kane.

Paired with Kuehne in round four, the three-time U.S. Amateur champion answered every challenge from the 22-year-old Texan. The tournament's defining moment occurred on the par-3 hole 7.

Inkster's drive cratered in a bunker. The lie made a par appear impossible and a bogey seem improbable. But Julie remembered a tip from Meg Mallon. "Keep the club face open, swing, but don't follow through."

The ball popped from the sand and settled on the lip of the cup. Inkster salvaged par, and Kuehne stood amazed.

Meanwhile, Kelli struggled with her putting. Of eight birdie chances on the front nine, the Dallas native converted only one.

Inkster, the 1984 LPGA Rookie of the Year who had not won a major championship in 10 years, birdied hole 13 and coasted to the win. Her final round of 71 bettered runner-up Sherri Turner by 5 strokes. Kuehne double-bogeyed the 18th to finish third, 6 strokes back. Juli's 16-under 272 set a U.S. Open record for the largest margin under par. Her four-day total bested Alison Nicholas' 10-under-par set in 1997.

When Inkster stood on the final tee, the former San Jose State golfer faced memories of the 1992 Open. She had led the field by

2 strokes heading into the final two holes. But Patty Sheehan birdied both 17 and 18 to force a playoff.

Sheehan's come-from-behind victory almost caused Juli to quit the professional tour. The native Californian suffered without a victory for four years and failed to break the top 20 in total winnings following the birth of her second daughter in 1994.

But a commitment to steady practice gradually brought Inkster to the top of her game. In both 1997 and 1998, she cracked the top ten in LPGA tour earnings. She had returned to her first love—golf.

Not only did Juli Inkster need to work hard, persevere, and play good golf, she also had to love the game in order to win. And even more special, two loves of her life, her daughters, watched the victory.

Jesus' beloved Apostle John penned much about love. In the New Testament Book of Revelation, he wrote about seven churches. He commended one, the Ephesians, for their hard work. He patted them on the back for their ability to see through phoniness. He applauded them for their perseverance.

But John judged them harshly because they had left their first love—Jesus Christ.

What or who is your first love? You may need to answer that question in categories. What person do you put first? What sport or hobby provides the most pleasure? Take a moment to let your first love know. Find some time for your favorite sport. But remember, no matter how much you treasure people or activities, God must come first. Confess the times He hasn't. Thank Him for forgiveness.

KELETI FINDS FREEDOM IN SPORTS

Now the Lord is the Spirit, and where the spirit of the Lord is, there is freedom. —2 CORINTHIANS 3:17

Adolf Hitler's war to enslave the world canceled the 1940 Olympics. But for 19-year-old Hungarian Agnes Keleti, the conflict resulted in much more than a lost medal opportunity.

Because of her Jewish faith, Keleti's gymnastics club expelled her in 1941. When the Nazis invaded Hungary, her entire family hid. The gymnast eluded capture by purchasing a forged set of papers from a Christian girl. She worked in a munitions factory and later as a maid for the deputy commandant of Budapest.

Keleti smuggled food to her mother and sister who lived in a safe house operated by Swedish humanitarian Raoul Wallenberg. They escaped harm, but her father was not as fortunate. He died in the gas chambers of Auschwitz.

After the war, Agnes returned to gymnastics. The Holocaust survivor made the 1948 Olympic squad but tore a ligament in her final training session and couldn't perform.

Four years later, Keleti debuted in the Olympics at age 31. In the games' first year of individual gymnastics competition, she stunned the field by capturing the gold in floor exercise, the silver in team competition, and bronzes in the uneven bars and the later discontinued portable apparatus team exercise.

The aging athlete believed her career had ended, but turbulent world events intervened once again. In 1956, the Hungarian fight against communism reached its peak. Gymnastics offered a means of escape.

Agnes tried out for the Olympic team and surprisingly made the squad at age 35. Even more astonishing at the Melbourne games, the victim of Nazi oppression claimed six medals, four gold and two silver. She captured firsts in three individual events—the floor exercise, the balance beam, and the uneven bars.

As Russian tanks rolled through Hungarian streets suppressing freedom, Keleti refused to return. She requested and received asylum in Australia. Eventually, the political refugee moved to Israel and became her adopted country's national gymnastics coach.

Agnes Keleti lived much of her life without freedom. But she found independence through her sport. No matter what was happening in the outside world, she surely felt unrestrained as she tumbled in the floor exercise and glided between the uneven bars. Finally she found true physical liberation during that last Olympics in which she competed.

Many people throughout the world live without physical freedom. Inmates live in prisons. Governments dictate religion, schooling, employment, and travel. Parents sell their daughters to work in other countries. In some cultures, choosing to follow Christ results in becoming an outcast, being imprisoned, or being executed.

But true freedom isn't physical. It's in the heart. Trusting Jesus brings freedom through the Holy Spirit. God offers liberty on the inside no matter what's happening in the outside world.

If you haven't already become a Christian, confess your need for the freedom from sin that God gives. Ask Christ to become your Savior as you trust in Him. If you are a Christian, share the freedom you have found in Jesus with a friend who doesn't yet know Him. Read about the courage of Christians who face persecution in other countries and pray for them.

Strengthen the feeble hands, steady the knees that give way; say to those with fearful hearts, "Be strong, do not fear." —ISAIAH 35:3-4

Harvard University holds a reputation as one of the world's great academic institutions. But on March 15, 1998, the Crimson shocked and astonished the world of women's basketball.

The school earned a berth in the NCAA tournament by posting a 22–4 record and winning the Ivy League crown. Officials regarded Harvard lightly, however, and seeded the team 16th in the West Regional.

The placement matched the Crimson against the number one-ranked Stanford Cardinal in the first round. At first glance, the game seemed a complete mismatch.

The Cardinals hosted the contest on their home court where they had won 59 consecutive games dating back to March 1994. Stanford possessed vast post-season experience with six Final Four appearances and two national titles in the 1990s.

But many overlooked that the top-rated team had lost two key players to injury. Kristin Folkl and Vanessa Nygaard both had torn ligaments in the season's final week and were unavailable for the NCAA tournament.

The depleted Stanford team struggled as senior forward Allison Feaster paced the Crimson offense. Her scoring and rebounding triggered Harvard to a 43–34 halftime lead.

Yet the hometown team refused to surrender quietly. The Cardinals narrowed the gap to lead 65–64 with a minute and a half to play.

Harvard rallied as junior forward Suzie Miller nailed a 16-foot jumper and put the Crimson back in front, 66–65. Miller followed with a 3-pointer from the left corner, and Feaster stole the ball in the final minute to seal the 71–67 triumph.

For the first time in NCAA basketball tournament history, a 16th seed had defeated a number one. Feaster, the nation's leading scorer, finished the game with 35 points and 13 rebounds.

The women from Harvard should have been afraid—afraid to play a number one seed, afraid to face a team with two national titles, afraid to step onto a court owned by their opponents. But they refused to be intimidated. They didn't tremble, shake, flinch, or shrink from the confrontation. They faced the challenge head-on. They overcame trembling hands and unsteady legs. And they won.

In life, it's easy to be afraid. Athletic opponents appear stronger and more able. Knees shake when standing before a group to speak or make a report. Palms sweat during tests of all kinds. Stomachs tie in knots of fear over broken friendships and difficult times.

But the Old Testament Prophet Isaiah gives good advice, "Be strong. Don't be afraid." Isaiah offers strength and steadiness. His assurance comes from God.

God doesn't promise victory in basketball or any other sport—though playing with strength and steadiness helps. He doesn't promise A-plusses on presentations and reports—though speaking with grace and assurance helps. He doesn't even promise restored relationships or smooth situations—though His presence and power help.

What God does promise is His support and His love.

Remember several situations that have made you afraid. They may be games, presentations, or simple life situations. Recall how you felt emotionally, physically, and spiritually. How did you handle your fear? Did it work? Thank God for the calm He offers.

He has performed mighty deeds with his arm; he has scattered those who are proud in their inmost thoughts. —LUKE 1:51

Joe Engel, owner of baseball's Chattanooga Lookouts of the Southern League, never missed an opportunity for outlandish promotion. The "Barnum of Baseball" staged elephant races, milking contests, and assorted other oddities to draw fans to his ballpark.

In the spring of 1931, Engel signed a 17-year-old pitcher named "Jackie" Mitchell. Ball clubs regularly inked promising rookies, but this youthful player seemed different. The full name on the contract between the Lookouts and the signee read, "Virnie Beatrice Mitchell."

Jackie possessed pinpoint control of her pitches. She threw a wicked curveball with a side-armed delivery that often deceived hitters.

The hopeful hurler claimed former Brooklyn Dodger Clarence "Dazzy" Vance taught her the mechanics of pitching. Mitchell furthered her diamond education by attending and graduating from ex-Yankee shortstop Norman "Kid" Elberfeld's baseball academy in Atlanta.

On April 2, the New York Yankees visited Chattanooga for an exhibition game. More than 4,000 fans along with scores of reporters, wire services, and a newsreel camera packed the stadium.

Clyde Barfoot started on the mound for Chattanooga but gave up a double and single to the first two batters. Lookout manager Bert Niehoff signaled for Jackie.

Yankee slugger Babe Ruth stepped into the box. Mitchell came at the home run hitter with her curve. The first pitch missed. Ruth swung mighty cuts at the next two, but his bat touched air.

After the Babe took Jackie's fourth pitch, the umpire bellowed, "Strike three! You're out!" The Sultan of Swat went through wild gyrations protesting the call before storming back to the New York dugout.

Mitchell then faced first baseman Lou Gehrig. The Iron Horse swung at three curveballs, missed them all, and silently strode to the bench.

A massive standing ovation greeted Jackie. She followed her strikeouts with a walk to Tony Lazzari before Niehoff reinserted Barfoot, legal under exhibition rules.

Several days later, Baseball Commissioner Kenesaw Mountain Landis voided Mitchell's contract stating baseball was "too strenuous" for women. Two years later, Jackie joined the House of David team and spent four years barnstorming across America before returning to Chattanooga.

Jackie Mitchell performed great feats with her pitching arm. That curve ball must have been something to see—or maybe not see—as it crossed the plate. And just imagine what two of baseball's greatest hitters must have thought as they stepped into the batter's box to face a woman.

"Soft tosser!" "A cinch hit!" "An easy homer!" "No girl can get me out!" surely echoed through their inner selves. But Jackie's arm prevailed as the umpire barked, "Strike three!"

In the Bible Book of Luke, Mary commended God for His mighty arm. She praised Him for dealing with the proud. The young mother-to-be rejoiced in the Mighty One choosing her to be the mother of the Savior Jesus.

Read Mary's song in Luke 2:46-55. Thank the Heavenly Father for the mighty blessings He has given you.

God's voice thunders in marvelous ways, he does great things beyond our understanding. He says to the snow, "Fall on the earth," and to the rain shower, "Be a mighty downpour." —JOB 37:5-6

No Bulgarian had ever won a Winter Olympics gold medal. In the 1998 Nagano games, the country's chances for breaking the streak appeared slim.

But coaches had forewarned every contestant that anything could happen in the biathlon. Circumstances proved their prediction correct.

The 1998 women's 15-kilometer competition took place in fresh, thick, heavy snow. A swirling wind blew falling snowflakes into the eyes of the athletes. The adverse weather conditions equaled the field.

The sport that combines Nordic cross-country skiing with rifle marksmanship requires extreme exertion coupled with a calm, steady hand. In the 15-K event, skiers stop at four different intervals to shoot 20 targets from more than 150 feet away.

Shots alternate from standing and prone positions. Each missed shot adds a minute to the total time. The winner must achieve near perfect balance.

Few expected Bulgaria's Yekaterina Dafovska to finish near the top. She ranked 51st in world competition upon her arrival in Japan.

But the 22-year-old athlete waxed her skis to an optimum level to take advantage of the fresh snow. She also paced her route with precision to obtain maximum skiing speed, minimal setup time, and accurate shooting. The Bulgarian missed only one of her 20 targets.

The 29th place finisher at the 1994 Lillehammer Games in Norway bolted to the gold with a time of 54:52.0. Another mid-

ranked competitor, Ukraine's Elena Petrova, garnered the silver, clocking a 55:09.8. Ursula Disl of Germany took bronze in 55:17.9. The pre-race favorite, Sweden's Magdelena Forsberg, finished a disappointing 14th after missing three targets.

Dafovska had dreamed that someday she would hear the Bulgarian national anthem played at the Winter Olympic games. She never imagined the notes would celebrate her gold medal as she stood atop the winner's stand.

But not only was Dafovska surprised at her victory, everyone else was as well. As exciting as it was, her win seemed beyond understanding, but the falling snow made the difference.

Sometimes we also find it hard to understand the wonder of God. He shows Himself through the natural world. He controls the sun and moon and stars. He makes grass grow and flowers bloom. He commands the rain to pour and the snow to fall. He makes the waves and the waters flow. He fashions each delicate, individual snowflake and fingerpaints the rainbow across the sky.

Yet, God cares about every person He has created. He counts the hairs on each head. He knows the thoughts in each mind and the feelings of each heart. He listens to the prayers of His followers and offers guidance and love.

The Heavenly Father's voice thunders and His touch reaches across the universe as His children experience His greatness. He is marvelous beyond all human understanding.

Spend some quiet time outside gazing at the beautiful world. Sing a hymn or praise song to the Creator of the Universe or read Psalm 104 as your prayer to the Almighty God.

NOVOTNA REDEEMED AT WIMBLEDON

*My lips will shout for joy when I sing praise to you—
I, whom you have redeemed.* —PSALM 71:23

Winning a Grand Slam event eluded Jana Novotna. In her only Australian Open final, she lost to Monica Seles. Twice she reached the Wimbledon finals, but the Czech star fell to Steffi Graf and Martina Hingis.

After her 1997 loss to Hingis, the Duchess of Kent assured Novotna three times would be the charm. In 1998, after dispatching Venus Williams in the quarterfinals and Hingis in the semis, the veteran player had an opportunity to prove the Duchess right.

The 29 year old faced France's Nathalie Tauziat, a 16th seed and relative unknown to most American tennis fans. But Tauziat owned a 4–4 career record against Novotna and hungered for a Grand Slam victory as much as her opponent did.

Jana started slowly and fell behind 2–0 in the first set. But the 13-year tour veteran refused to panic and broke Tauziat's serve to tie, 2–2.

The three-time Grand Slam runner-up broke the French woman's serve again with an overhand slam and went up 4–3. Each player held over the next three games, and Novotna claimed set one, 6–4.

In set two, Wimbledon's third seed built an apparent insurmountable 5–3 margin, but the 30-year-old Tauziat battled back to go ahead 6–5. However, Jana remained calm, held serve, and forced a tiebreaker.

With the match on the line, the French woman disintegrated. Her Czech opponent landed strong serves, and Tauziat responded with a volley of errors. Novotna took the tiebreaker 7–2 to claim the match and silver tray awarded Wimbledon's champion.

Following match point, the first-time champion fell to her knees and burst into tears. After embracing Nathalie, she scam-

pered into the stands to hug her mother Liba and her coach Hana Mandlikova.

Novotna then joined the Duchess at Center Court for a jubilant presentation. She held her trophy high and cried for joy.

Jana Novotna had broken through. The perpetual runner-up had finally won. A flood of emotions cascaded through her mind and body—elation, excitement, exuberance, exhaustion, and enjoyment. She felt sheer relief. The win redeemed her losses.

The champion's body, face, and voice made the victory evident. Anyone could have tuned the television channel to the celebration and identified the winner.

God gives us victory in life. He rescues us from sin and its penalties. In theological terms, He redeems us.

But can people who see us tell? If they tuned to the television channel showing our story, would they know? Do we live life with shouts of joy and praises to God on our lips? Do we celebrate our Heavenly Father and hold the trophy of our salvation high?

The psalmist did.

Enjoy a game of tennis with a friend or hit a few balls against a backboard. If you make a poor shot, redeem yourself by making a better one. Think about the biblical meaning of redemption. Celebrate the prize of your salvation. Praise God.

USA BANNER CARRIED BY FIVE-TIME OLYMPIAN

*We will shout for joy when you are victorious
and lift up our banners in the name of our God.*

—PSALM 20:5

The Olympic Opening Ceremonies provide some of sports' most colorful and majestic moments. Athletes and flags from virtually every nation parade in splendor. Thousands in person and millions via television witness the spectacular event.

Carrying a country's banner represents the highest honor an Olympic team can bestow. In 1992, the United States selected a popular but little known athlete.

Francie Larrieu-Smith joined the United States track team in 1969 at age 16. She experienced modest success until Coach Augie Argabright convinced her to focus on the middle distance races.

During her teens and twenties, Larrieu-Smith ran every event from the 1,000 meters to the 3,000 meters. The sixth born of nine children qualified for both the 1972 and 1976 Olympic 1,500-meter teams but failed to medal. She earned a third berth on the 1980 squad but never competed due to the United States boycott.

As Francie entered her thirties, she switched to longer distances. In 1988, she claimed a spot on the Olympic 10,000-meter roster and placed a surprising fifth in the Seoul (South Korea) Games.

At the 1992 Barcelona (Spain) Games, Larrieu-Smith competed in the marathon, finishing in the number 12 slot. As a five-time Olympian, fellow Americans honored Francie by selecting her as the United States flag bearer for the Opening Ceremony.

Knee problems ultimately forced Francie to retire from active marathon competition. She completed a master's degree in sports administration at the University of Texas and began coaching men's and women's cross country track at Southwestern University in Georgetown, Texas.

Just imagine how Francie Larrieu-Smith felt when she learned that her fellow United States Olympians had voted her the one to carry the flag. Think of the chill she experienced as she waited in the tunnel in Barcelona with all the American athletes lined up behind her.

Picture the crowd cheering as Francie appeared on the track holding high the Stars and Stripes. Visualize the mist in her eyes and the lump in her throat as she proudly waved the banner and led the Red, White, and Blue Team around the arena. What an incredible experience!

Then, think about carrying God's banner. Picture yourself waving His symbol before thousands of people. Visualize the cheering crowd and shouts of joy for the victorious Christ. What an incredible experience!

But carrying God's banner isn't left to your imagination. You lift it high through your words, your actions, and your life. You wave His symbol every day.

Take a good look at the American flag. Note the seven red and six white stripes signifying the 13 original colonies. Admire the 50 bright white stars, one for every state, displayed against a brilliant blue canton. Recall the meaning of the colors chosen from the hues of Great Britain's Union Jack. Charles Thomson, Secretary of the Continental Congress, related that "White signifies purity and innocence, red, hardiness and valour, and blue . . . signifies vigilance, perseverence, and justice." Praise God for what the Stars and Stripes symbolize. Ask the Lord to help you be a visible banner for Him.

Listen to my cry for help, my King and my God, for to you I pray. —PSALM 5:2

Allison Beightol chose Randolph-Macon College because of its size, proximity to home, and willingness to let her and her twin sister play both basketball and soccer. The NCAA Division III athlete enjoyed great success in both sports but won her most significant award for unselfish acts of sportsmanship.

The Randolph-Macon Yellow Jacket basketball team traveled to Salem, Virginia, to face their arch-rival Roanoke College Maroons. The Yellow Jackets had previously defeated the Maroons at home, 75–69, handing the visitors their only conference loss.

Roanoke desperately wanted to even the series and move into a tie for the 1999 Old Dominion Athletic Conference lead. But the Maroons committed 17 first half turnovers, and the Yellow Jackets led at intermission, 29–19.

The Maroons cut the lead to 2 in the second half. But while Roanoke attempted a fast break, Allison's twin sister, Aimee, broke up the downcourt pass and collided with the Maroon's Suzanne Webb.

The ball popped free into Allison's hands and created an open fast break on the opposite end for the Yellow Jackets. Suddenly Allison called time-out before her team could shoot.

Through the noise and confusion, she had heard Suzanne cry out in agony. Allison chose to forego the easy basket in a tight game in order that a competitor receive prompt medical attention.

As the clock ticked down, Randolph-Macon climbed ahead by 11, leading 70–59. In the remaining seconds, Roanoke inserted senior Alexis Riseman.

Before play resumed, Allison huddled the team around her. She reminded her teammates that this game honored the Maroons' seniors. Riseman had received little playing time her final year due to injuries on both knees. Since the outcome had been decided, the senior guard asked the other Yellow Jackets to avoid contact and let the Roanoke senior shoot.

Carroll LaHaye, Randolph-Macon's coach, nominated Allison Beightol for the NCAA's inaugural Outstanding Sportpersons of the Year Award. She received the honor at the Citizenship Through Sports Alliance meeting in Washington, D.C., on June 29, 1999.

The award-winner did the unexpected. Allison performed in a way unusual for today's athlete. She treated an opponent with kindness. She heard Suzanne's cries for help, and she responded.

Then Beightol once again did the abnormal. She put herself in the place of an injured star playing possibly her final home game at far less than her full, athletic strength. She treated an opponent with empathy. She saw the look on Alexis' face, and she responded.

Unfortunately in today's athletics, competition often outweighs kindness, and urgency frequently outweighs empathy. True sportsmanship gets lost in the enthusiasm of winning and the bitterness of defeat.

But God desires that, like Allison, we hear the cries of our opponents just as He listens to us. And then He asks us, like Allison, to go one step farther and respond. After all, He does.

Think about the meaning of sportsmanship. Try to recall some examples you have seen. If you were writing the guidelines for the NCAA Outstanding Sportpersons of the Year Award, what would they be? Confess to God times when you haven't been a very good sport. Ask Him to help you remember to act like a Christian, even in competition.

GEORGIA DEPTH BRINGS HOME SWIMMING TITLE

Oh, the depth of the riches of the wisdom and knowledge of God! —ROMANS 11:33

The University of Georgia hosted the 1999 NCAA Women's Swimming and Diving Championships at the Gabrielsen Natatorium. The Bulldogs had never won the title and fervently hoped to showcase their talent for the faithful home fans.

Georgia's swimmers failed to capture top honors in any event on the opening day of the three-day competition. But the home team's depth vaulted it into first place, 6 points ahead of Southern Methodist University.

On day two, the Bulldogs' individual stars began to shine. Junior Kristy Kowal claimed Georgia's first gold medal.

The reigning world 100-meter breaststroke champion won first place in her specialty with a time of 59.25 seconds. She added another gold in the 200-meter breaststroke, setting a new NCAA mark of 2:07.66. The native of Wymossing, Pennsylvania, received the Swimmer of the Meet award for her double victories and collegiate record.

Further first place finishes eluded Georgia until the competition had almost ended. But consistent performances in the top eight spots kept the school atop the overall standings.

On the final day, Julie Varozza gave the Bulldogs a great boost with a surprise triumph in the 1,650-meter freestyle. Her winning time of 15:59.66 bested the nearest competitor by almost 5 seconds.

Keegan Walkley provided the meet's biggest upset. Her 1:53.63 victory in the 200-meter backstroke over defending champion Misty Hyman of Stanford clinched Georgia's first national swimming and diving title.

When the scoresheets had been tallied, the Bulldogs totaled 504

1/2 points compared to 441 for defending champion Stanford. In addition to the four first places, Georgia claimed three seconds, three thirds and fourteen fourths, fifths, sixth, sevenths, and eighths. The home team failed to garner points in only five of the meet's twenty-one events.

Although Kristy Kowal's medals captured the crowd, the Georgia Lady Bulldogs didn't win the NCAA Swimming and Diving Championship with outstanding individual performances. They didn't even add to the score with relay golds.

Instead the women won with depth. Almost every swimmer and diver contributed at least a few points in one event or another. Team members gave their best efforts to place. Every place counted, and in the end, the count totaled victory.

God's church is that way. Every individual has a gift to contribute and a role in the congregation. Some preach. Some teach. Some encourage and comfort. Others sing. Many minister. A few keep the building clean or show hospitality. Still more visit and provide food for those in need. All should pray and give.

God doesn't measure success in His church by individual achievement. He doesn't even award points for fame of the pastor, number of members, size of building, or value of property and furnishings. Instead, God determines success in His churches by depth—the depth of commitment, the depth of worship, and the depth of involvement in bringing others to know Christ.

Examine the depth of your church. Read Saint Paul's whole doxology in Romans 11:33-36. Note that doxology means a hymn or verse of praise to God. Praise God for the riches found in the depth of His wisdom and knowledge and for the depth of possibilities in your church.

AKERS MOVES FROM FATIGUE TO MVP

*Let us not become weary in going good, for at the
proper time we will reap a harvest if we do not give up.
Therefore, as we have opportunity, let us do good to all people,
especially to those who belong to the family of believers.*

—GALATIANS 6:9-10

As a young girl, Michelle Akers dreamed of playing
football for the Pittsburgh Steelers. Her fantasy soon met
with reality, and she turned to soccer instead.

Michelle earned a scholarship to the University of Central
Florida where she won All-American honors four times. In 1985,
she joined the United States National Soccer Team and played a
major role in elevating her country to the top of international
competition.

As a warm-up for the 1996 Olympic games, America hosted
Canada, Japan, and China in the U.S. Women's Cup. The four
teams competed in the round robin tournament. Both the United
States and China defeated Canada and Japan. The Americans and
Chinese met in the Cup finals.

A sparse crowd of 6,081 attended the event held in
Washington, D.C.'s RFK Stadium, but ESPN broadcast the game
live. The telecast marked the first time the United States women's
soccer team had been viewed by a national audience.

The contest's low scoring and tenacious defense typified all previous United States–China confrontations. Although the
Americans outshot the Chinese, the host country failed to score in
the first half.

In the game's 63rd minute Akers dribbled past two defenders
and blasted the ball into the net. The 1–0 score held, and the
United States soccer team captured its third consecutive U.S.
Women's Cup. Officials selected Michelle as both the final game's
and tournament's Most Valuable Player.

For Akers, the honors represented the pinnacle of a long comeback. In September 1993, the soccer star learned she suffered from Epstein-Barr Virus, commonly known as Chronic Fatigue Syndrome. Following a lengthy recovery, Michelle suffered a severe knee injury in the opening five minutes of the 1995 World Cup and didn't play again until the team's semifinal loss to Norway.

But Michelle Akers never gave up. On days when she was weary and wanted to stay in bed, she got up. At times when she didn't feel like rehabilitating that knee, she kept at it. When she became discouraged, she fought through her feelings.

No crowd cheered the soccer player's effort, but her hard, lonely work finally paid off. Michelle helped bring home a team victory and earned individual honors.

Sometimes as Christians we grow weary. We become tired of doing good. We face discouragement when our efforts go unnoticed and unappreciated. We wonder if right living and helping others really pays off.

But God assures us that if we continue doing good, we'll reap our deserved harvest. He encourages us to do our best, to be genuine, generous, loving, and kind to all people, especially to other Christians.

And even if the reward doesn't come on earth, the Lord will surely give it in heaven.

Look up the word "good" in a collegiate or unabridged dictionary. Apply as many of the numerous definitions as you can to your Christian life. Think of one way that you can practice doing good in one day. Then do it. Ask God to help you not grow weary in doing good. Praise Him for the rewards He gives.

AUSTRALIAN NAMED COLLEGE LACROSSE USA'S PLAYER OF THE YEAR

Consequently, you are no longer foreigners and aliens, but fellow citizens with God's people and members of God's household. —EPHESIANS 2:19

Jen Adams learned of the University of Maryland's women's lacrosse team long before the Brighton, Australia native left her homeland. Fellow countrywoman Sascha Newmarch had joined the Terrapin squad three years earlier.

As a young girl, Adams watched Newmarch in action. When Sascha journeyed to America, every lacrosse fan in South Australia began following Maryland's fortunes. Jen readily accepted an offer to join a fellow Aussie in the United States.

The trans-Pacific player made an immediate impact on the team. As a freshman, she started every game at striker, scoring 44 points on 27 goals and 17 assists.

Despite two conference losses and a fourth seed in the Atlanta Coast Conference Tournament, the Terps drew upon vast experience and advanced to the 1998 NCAA finals for the fourth straight year. An 11–5 victory over Virginia brought Maryland its fifth championship trophy.

With a year of experience, Jen improved unbelievably. In 21 games, the sophomore scored 117 points on 71 goals and 46 assists. Her efforts broke both of Kelly Amonte's 1996 school records of 62 goals and 110 points.

Surprisingly, Adams' passing ability and not her shooting skill paved the way for her record-setting season. Her unselfish team play set up numerous scoring opportunities for both her and her teammates.

In 1999, Maryland carried a perfect 20–0 record into the NCAA Championship game against Virginia. The twice-beaten Cavaliers hoped for an upset, but their aspirations soon shattered.

The Terrapins scored 4 goals in the first 10 minutes and closed the half on a 5–0 run to lead 11–2 at intermission. Maryland opened the second half with five uncontested goals and cruised to a 16–6 triumph.

With the victory, the perennial lacrosse powerhouse extended its winning streak to 28 games and captured its sixth NCAA Championship and fifth in a row. The school also matched its undefeated 1995 and 1996 seasons with a mark of 21–0.

In the championship contest, Jen scored 4 goals and gathered an assist while winning Tournament Most Valuable Player honors. The following month, *College Lacrosse USA* named her NCAA Division I Player of the Year.

It didn't take long for Australian Jen Adams to be accepted by the coaches and lacrosse players at the University of Maryland. Because of the athlete's talent and unselfishness, teammates no longer saw her as a foreigner but as a fellow player and member of the Terrapin squad. They felt at home with each other.

People from other countries sometimes seem different or alien. They may dress differently. They eat different foods and speak different languages. Even if they do know English, their accents sound funny and their word choices seem strange.

But God created every person everywhere. We all belong to the Creator. We are His children. When we love the Father and accept Him through faith in Jesus Christ, we join God's household. We become citizens of His kingdom.

If you don't know much about lacrosse, watch a game or read about the sport in an encyclopedia or on the internet. Note that lacrosse enjoys more popularity in countries outside the United States. As you meet international students or foreign visitors in your community or while on vacation, pay special attention to making them feel at home. Ask God to help you see them as part of His family.

BROTHER'S DEATH MOTIVATES BRISCO-HOOKS

Death has climbed in through our windows and has entered our fortresses; it has cut off the children from the streets and the young men from the public squares.

—JEREMIAH 9:21

In 1974, 18-year-old Robert Brisco died from a stray bullet fired as he ran on the Los Angeles Locke High School track. His 14-year-old sister Valerie grieved greatly over the passing of her role model.

The teenage girl channeled her energies and frustrations into running. Track and field observers took note of the young woman in 1977 when she clocked a 54.19 in the 400 meters. In 1979, the surprising sprinter dropped to 52.08 seconds, her fastest time for the next five years.

In 1981, Valerie married Alvin Hooks, a California State at Northridge football player. The couple had a son, Alvin Hooks, Jr., in 1982.

The Greenwood, Mississippi, native who had moved to Los Angeles at age six, gained 40 pounds during her pregnancy. To lose the weight and recondition, Valerie wrapped her body in cellophane and ran in place in her bathroom with hot water steaming off the tile.

The transplanted Californian shocked track fans by qualifying for the 1984 Los Angeles Olympics in the 200 and 400 meters. But the 24 year old would perform even more amazing feats when the eyes of the world focused on the summer games.

In the first event, the 400 meters, oddsmakers favored Chandra Cheeseborough whose come-from-behind victory defeated Valerie in the Olympic trials. But in the run for the gold, the dark horse held off Cheeseborough's finishing kick and set an Olympic record of 48.83 seconds in her winning effort.

Three days later, Brisco-Hooks, aided by the absence of East

Germany's Marita Koch and Marlies Gohr, overcame a poor start and bolted to a second gold and Olympic record of 21.81. Her victories in both the 200 and 400 meters preceded Michael Johnson's Atlanta Olympics double win by 12 years.

Valerie captured her third gold medal as a member of the 4 x 400 relay, making her the first female to accomplish the feat since Wilma Rudolph in 1960. Her record-setting performances occurred fewer than three miles from the site of her beloved brother's death.

Robert Brisco's memory inspired his sister to Olympic track glory. She felt her brother's presence in her spirit even though she couldn't touch him physically. Death had intruded into the Brisco's family.

Old people are supposed to die, not teenagers. Sick people are supposed to pass away, not healthy runners. School campuses are supposed to be secure, not places where bullets spray. But death doesn't always happen that way, and schools aren't always safe. God allowed the Brisco family to be affected by the sinful choices of others. Robert died because of the decision made by the one who fired the gun.

And while God is always in control, He does not control our choices. That's up to us. Valerie Brisco-Hooks made a choice. She could have decided to become bitter over her brother's death. Instead she chose to use his end as a positive beginning for her life. That's what God wants us to do.

Examine a daily newspaper or watch the television news. Look for examples of violence caused by the sinful decisions of people. Choose one story and pray for the victims. Ask God to help them through their difficult days, to take away their bitterness, and to let them use the bad for good in their lives .

"Rise and thresh, O Daughter of Zion, for I will give you horns of iron; I will give you hoofs of bronze and you will break to pieces many nations." —MICAH 4:13

In the 1980s, Coach Jody Conradt built the University of Texas Lady Longhorns into one of the nation's top women's basketball teams. But despite stellar records in 1983, 1984, and 1985, each season ended with a gut-wrenching loss in the NCAA regionals.

A senior-laden squad committed to a championship in 1986. After escaping with a 2-point victory over Ohio State in the season opener, the Lady Horns rolled to victory after victory.

UT entered Southwest Conference play with an unblemished 8–0 mark. Conradt's charges crushed every conference opponent and began post-season action with a perfect 29–0 record.

Austin hosted the Midwest Regional at the Erwin Center. After routing Oklahoma, 85–59, and edging Ole Miss, 66–53, on their home floor, the Lady Horns advanced to their first Final Four.

Texas drew Western Kentucky in the semifinals. The previous year, the Lady Hilltoppers upset UT, 92–90, sending them packing from the Mideast Regional. But in the rematch, the Texans exacted revenge, whipping their opponents, 90–65.

Two-time champion University of Southern California represented the final obstacle on the Lady Longhorns' quest. Four-time All-American Cheryl Miller paced the USC Women of Troy.

But UT's defense put the clamps on the USC forward. Freshman Clarissa Davis drew the assignment of battling Miller when Annette Smith incurred two fouls within the first five minutes.

Davis held the All-American to 2 baskets in 11 attempts. Miller finished the contest with 16 points before fouling out with 7:30 remaining.

In addition to her glue-like guarding and 14 rebounds, the

Lady Longhorn freshman sparkled on offense. Clarissa led all UT scorers with 24 points, going 9-for-14 from the field and 6-for-8 from the line.

Davis captured the Final Four MVP Award as Texas easily defeated Southern Cal, 97–81. The Lady Horns became the fourth women's basketball team to complete an undefeated season.

The University of Texas women rose from the disappointment of previous seasons to defeat every rival. Lady Horn Clarissa Davis broke Lady Trojan Cheryl Miller's effectiveness for that final win. The NCAA Women's Championship capped a rare season. The UT ladies were amazing. They were perfect.

In the Book of Micah, God promises similar victory to His people. He says they will break down their enemies. The Lord doesn't insure daily life will be easy. He doesn't guarantee there won't be defeats or disappointments along the way. He doesn't warrant that we will be perfect—except through His perfection.

But the Heavenly Father does pledge ultimate triumph as part of His plan for His followers for eternity.

Imagine what it would be like to play on a team that never loses—that ends its season with a perfect record. Think about breaking down every opponent. Reflect on the meaning of the word perfect. Name some things in your life that seem perfect or almost perfect. Remember that only God is truly perfect in all ways at all times. Praise Him.

MARY JO PEPPLER SUPERSTAR

> *Is not God in the heights of heaven? And see how
> lofty are the highest stars?* —JOB 22:12

Mary Jo Peppler earned spots on both the 1964 and
1968 United States Olympic volleyball teams. But neither
squad fared well against tough international competition.

Although Peppler's American clubs consistently captured AAU
national championships, the United States Volleyball Association
considered Mary Jo a renegade. Despite being voted the world's
best woman volleyball player in 1970, the USVBA refused her a
1976 Olympic berth as either a player or coach. But a made-for-
television event created a venue for the outstanding athlete to
showcase her talent.

The ABC Network organized "The Superstars" and brought
together eleven top American female athletes. In addition to
Peppler, the participants included skier Kiki Cutter, surfer Laura
Ching, speed skater Diane Holum, softball pitcher Joan Joyce,
bowler Paula Sperber, gymnast Kathy Rigby, football player
Barbara O'Brien, sprinter Wyomia Tyus, basketball player Karen
Logan, and diver Micki King.

Each contestant selected seven of ten events for competition,
and none could choose a skill from her own sport. Peppler opted
for free-throw shooting, softball throwing, the 60-yard dash, the
440-yard dash, cycling, rowing, and swimming.

On the first day, she took second in cycling, fourth in the 60,
and fifth in both the 440 and swimming. No one considered the
volleyball player a serious contender for the Superstar title.

But day two dawned differently for Mary Jo. She claimed three
first places in the remaining free-throw shooting, softball throwing, and rowing to edge out Karen Logan 41–38. Micki King
placed third with 36.

For her efforts, the 1960s Olympian earned $34,100. That

amount represented ten times more money than Peppler had made the prior year as a professional volleyball player.

Mary Jo Peppler won the title Superstar over ten other women considered to be superior athletes in her day. She showed she could reach the same lofty heights they could and move beyond them. Her star burned highest and brightest, at least for that competition during that week.

God made Mary Jo Peppler, and God made the stars that shine in the heights of heaven. They twinkle so high in the universe that we can scarcely imagine the distance. They glow with such power that we can't fathom the fire. They burn holes so far across the night sky that we must lie on the ground or lean our heads backward to glimpse their glory. They sprinkle in such varied patterns we study books to learn their names.

To God, Mary Jo Peppler is just one of the many stars He has created among His people. As each heavenly body adds its light to the night sky, so each person adds a special glow to God's world. Some burn with more power than others. Some possess more memorable names. Some seem nearer or farther away. But every one is a superstar, God's superstar.

Spend some time enjoying the stars. Use an astronomy book or encyclopedia to learn the names of the major constellations and brightest stars. Look through a telescope or visit an observatory or planetarium. Praise God for the stars. Ask the Heavenly Father to help your life shine brightly for Him.

SKATER JANET LYNN EARNS REWARD

*"May the Lord repay you for what you have done.
May you be richly rewarded by the Lord, the God of
Israel, under whose wings you have come to take refuge."*

—RUTH 2:12

Janet Lynn Nowicki had to be forced onto the floor
for her dancing lessons. But the two year old taught herself to ice skate at her very first outing.

At age four, her parents moved to Rockford, Illinois, so that
Janet could train at the Wagon Wheel Figure Skating Club. Her
coach, Slavka Kohout, shortened Nowicki's performing name to
Janet Lynn and transformed a shy, chubby youngster into a grace-
ful, confident performer.

The former Junior National Champion showcased her talents on
the international scene at age 14 in the 1968 Winter Olympics in
Grenoble, France. The following year Janet reeled off her first of
five consecutive United States Figure Skating titles.

The American earned a second berth on the 1972 United States
Olympic squad. But the free-spirited Janet always struggled
against world-class competition.

At that time, the compulsory figures comprised 50 percent of
the skater's final score. In 1991, too late for Janet, the
International Skating Union eliminated them entirely.

Lynn considered the painstaking patterns dreadful drudgery
and performed them accordingly. Despite her breathtaking free
skate routines and first places in that part of the competition, she
often had to settle for less than gold.

The 1972 Sapporo (Japan) Games proved no different. Austria's
Beatrix Schuba built a huge lead in the school figures while Janet
lagged far behind.

But in the free skate portion, Lynn floated, danced, and spun
across the ice, wearing the biggest of smiles. At the conclusion of

her performance, the Japanese honored the American with their greatest display of respect—a totally silent arena.

Schuba, who placed seventh in free skating, claimed the gold medal, however, because of Janet's uninspired compulsory win. Canada's Karen Magnussen placed second, and Janet settled for bronze. The normally stoic Sapporo crowd jeered the decision.

In 1973, Janet Lynn Nowicki turned professional. Citing the opportunity to serve God and help others, the American signed a three-year, $1.4 million contract with the Shipstads and Johnson Ice Follies. With the stroke of her pen, Janet became the world's highest paid female athlete.

Initially, it all felt so unfair. The young woman's terrific talent on the ice seemed overshadowed by mechanical and archaic requirements. The inspired skater rarely won. The perfectly precise, sometimes wooden, performer usually did.

But ultimately Janet received her reward, not in gold medals but in pure gold. She was repaid for all she had done. In turn, she used her wealth wisely.

In the Bible, Boaz wished the same for Ruth. But he wasn't referring to gold. He talked of life. He knew God would reward Ruth for all the good she had done and the kindness she had shown. Ruth married into Boaz's wealthy family, and she gave her life to the Lord in return. Our Savior Jesus was one of her descendants.

Read about the history of skating in an encyclopedia or on the Internet. Either on ice or on the ground, trace the intricate compulsory figures. Then think about the other kind of figures, monetary figures, Janet Lynn received as her reward. What would you do with $1.4 million dollars? What kind of good could you do with it? Ask God to help you wisely use your wealth of time and money.

DAVENPORT POWERS TO WIN U.S. OPEN

As a junior United States Open champion, Lindsay Davenport appeared to have unlimited potential. But the expected championships never materialized when the California native became a professional tennis player.

A gold medal victory in the 1996 summer Olympics sparked Davenport's game. She lost weight. She gained strength and gradually climbed in the rankings.

By 1998, the American had risen to number two on the WTA tour. In the United States Open that year, Lindsay blew past Amanda Coetzer in the quarterfinals and survived a three-set, two-tie breaker match with Venus Williams in the semis.

Davenport faced 17-year-old Martina Hingis, the defending Open champion and winner of four Grand Slam titles, in the finals. The once struggling 22 year old had never advanced past the semifinals in any previous Grand Slam appearance. The experience felt new to her.

The Olympic gold medalist used her 6-foot 2-inch frame to great advantage against her Swiss opponent. Lindsay's ballistic baseline volleys hugged the boundaries so tightly Hingis could do nothing but stare and glare.

In the first set, Davenport twice broke her opponent's serve. At 1–1, she nailed a brutal backhand for game point, and at 4–1 took the game with a wicked inside-out forehand. The Californian won the set, 6–3, closing with a backhand down the line that left Martina dead in her tracks.

But Davenport tightened, and the number-one ranked player went up 5–4 in the second set. Lindsay drew upon her newly found confidence and returned three straight winners. Hingis double faulted to tie, 5–5.

The former junior champion held serve and forged ahead 6–5. In the next game, she claimed match point by retrieving Martina's drop shot and pasting it crosscourt with a winning backhand. Davenport became the first American to hold the U. S. crown since Chris Evert captured the title in 1982.

What power! Just imagine the velocity of a tennis ball hit by a woman 6-feet, 2-inches tall. In those hands, the racquet became a tool to earn her a victory and the honor and exaltation that accompany a Grand Slam title. And how exciting that a United States citizen finally won the U.S. Open after sixteen years.

That day, Lindsay Davenport ruled the court and the women's tennis world. But every day God rules the whole world. His hands hold strength and power. He controls all wealth and apportions all honor.

He is God, and we are not. We hold only earthly power in our hands. Our strength diminishes with age. Worldly honors slip away. Exaltation fades into everydayness and rarely lives long past our death.

But God is God. He holds the universe in His hands. He rules!

Name as many current earthly rulers as you can. Include kings, queens, presidents, prime ministers, emperors, and other heads of state. Note that they have different amounts of power within their own countries. How much influence do they possess after they leave office or position? Praise God for His power. Thank Him for ruling wisely over all the earth.

TINY KENYAN RUNS TALL

Saul answered, "But am I not a Benjamite, from the smallest tribe of Israel, and is not my clan the least of all the clans of the tribe of Benjamin? Why do you say such a thing to me?" —1 SAMUEL 9:21

Tegla Loroupe stands only 4-feet, 11-inches tall and weighs just 85 pounds. But when the 26-year-old Kenyan runs, she rises head and shoulders above the crowd.

As a young girl, the men of her Bokot tribe discouraged Loroupe's running efforts. Tegla ignored them knowing God had given her a plan, and no man could alter it.

Her parents also offered little support. They believed a female's activities should be limited to cooking, keeping house, and caring for children.

Growing up on a vast cattle ranch kept the African girl in tremendous shape. Often while rounding up the animals, she chased the herd for more than 12 miles.

Eventually, Loroupe traveled abroad to pursue her athletic dreams. Anne Roberts, coordinator for the New York City Marathon, discovered Tegla in Germany and invited her to participate in the prestigious event.

The native of Kapenguria, a village 400 miles from Nairobi, caught the eye of the running world with her victory in the 1994 New York showcase. She returned to the Big Apple for an encore triumph in 1995.

World record holder, Ingrid Kristiansen, met Loroupe at the 1996 New York Marathon and told the Kenyan she would someday break her mark. After Tegla won the 1997 Rotterdam race in 2 hours, 22 minutes, and 7 seconds (2:22:07), racing fans believed the day would soon arrive.

The following year, Tegla competed once again at Rotterdam. At the 30-kilometer point, Loroupe lagged behind Kristiansen's pace.

But the Kenyan finished the final 12 kilometers in 40:48, making up over a minute.

She completed the 26-mile, 385-yard Rotterdam course in 2:20:47. Her time bettered Kristiansen's April 1985 mark of 2:21:06 by 19 seconds. The Norwegian's record had stood for thirteen years, longer than any previous marathoner's top time—either male or female. But Tegla Loroupe had broken it.

Tegla could certainly seem lost standing next to the other marathoners at the beginning of the race. Many towered over her by a foot or more. Probably in the beginning, some made fun of her tiny frame.

And then she had to overcome stereotypes held by her family and culture. They believed girls shouldn't do anything outside the home, regardless of talent or ambition.

But the young Kenyan offered no excuses. She didn't let her size get in the way. She didn't let stereotypes stop her. She took God's plan and ran with it.

In the Bible, Saul did offer excuses. When Judge Samuel approached the young Benjamite about being anointed King of Israel, he hesitated. Though tall himself, Saul belonged to the smallest and least important tribe of the nation. When the time came for the new king to be presented to the people, he hid among the baggage. Saul reigned as the reluctant king.

When the King of Kings calls us, do we offer excuses? Do we say we are too small or weak? Do we refuse Him or accept only grudgingly? Instead, the Lord desires that we take His plan and run with it.

Read the story of Saul becoming king in 1 Samuel 8:19–10:24. Examine your response to God when His holy nudges move you in a new direction. Ask the Lord to help you pursue His plan—willingly.

Water Play Keeps Se Ri Pak in U.S. Open Contention

Who has measured the waters in the hollow of his hand, or with the breadth of his hand marked off the heavens? Who has held the dust of the earth in a basket, or weighed the mountains on the scales and the hills in a balance? —ISAIAH 40:12

Golf fans had never witnessed a tournament like the 1998 United States Women's Open. After four regulation rounds, South Korea's Se Ri Pak and Duke University amateur Jenny Chausiriporn tied at 290, 6-over-par.

LPGA officials scheduled an 18-hole playoff the following day. Chausiriporn, whose parents immigrated to the United States from Thailand, quickly moved into a 4-stroke lead with three birdies on the first five holes. But her triple-bogey on the par-3 number six cut the margin to a single stroke.

From that point forward, the pair of 20-year-old golfers battled stroke-for-stroke. Pak and Chausiriporn approached the 18th hole of their playoff round knotted at 1-over-par. The South Korean hit a horrendous shot off the tee that rolled onto a water hazard bank while the Duke University senior kept her drive in the fairway. Pak, knowing a drop and the resulting penalty stroke would cost her the title, elected to swing away.

The first-year golf pro who began playing in 1989 doffed her shoes and socks. She stood barefoot in the water and wedged the ball over the 6-foot bank and to the right hand rough, 138 yards from the pin.

Se Ri then hit an 8-iron and placed her ball 17 feet from the hole. Her putt for par fell short by almost a foot.

Meanwhile, Jenny's second shot landed on the fringe of the green, 50 feet from the pin. Her first putt rolled 15 feet short. With the pressure on, she pushed her second putt just slightly, and the ball slid past the hole.

Both golfers settled for bogies and remained tied after 90 holes. According to the rules, play moved to a sudden death format.

Pak and Chausiriporn both parred the first playoff hole. On the second, each competitor reached the green in 2 strokes, but the collegian missed her birdie putt. She could only watch as the South Korean sank an 18-footer.

Se Ri Pak won, but it had taken 92 holes. Really, she gave herself the opportunity for victory because of her water play on the 18th hole. Wading into the wet and muddy hazard took a measure of courage. But she weighed her options and decided taking off her shoes and socks was the only way.

The Prophet Isaiah tells about one who measures the water in a different way, in the hollow of His hand. He talks about one who uses that same hand to mark off the heavens and gather the earth's dirt into mountains and hills.

Isaiah tells about God. God cares that we have fresh water to drink. He looks after the rich soil that grows crops for food. He provides hillsides for livestock grazing. His concern spans the highest mountain and the deepest valley.

But the Lord expects us to consider the world too. He desires that we treat the environment with respect and caution. He asks that we care for the water and land.

It's His gift and our responsibility.

Find out the source of the water you drink. Notice in the grocery store where the fruits and vegetables you eat are grown. Think about ways you can preserve the environment. Praise God for His wonderful earth. Ask Him to help you protect it.

COURTESY LPGA

COURTESY RANDOLPH-MACON COLLEGE

TOP *Kelli Kuehne battles the courses and diabetes on the LPGA tour.* (SEE PAGE 24)

BOTTOM *Allison Beightol's sportsmanship brings NCAA recognition.* (SEE PAGE 64)

Lindsay Davenport's powerful strokes win 1998 U. S. Open. (SEE PAGE 80)

COURTESY TRAVIS HATFIELD / UNIVERSITY OF GEORGIA

COURTESY PENN STATE UNIVERSITY

TOP *Kristy Kowal leads the University of Georgia to swimming gold.* (SEE PAGE 66)

BOTTOM *Suzie McConnell Serio achieves WNBA stardom after becoming the mother of four children.* (SEE PAGE 94)

COURTESY LPGA

COURTESY TRAVIS HATFIELD / UNIVERSITY OF GEORGIA

TOP *Betsy King reigns on the LPGA tour.* (SEE PAGE 136)

BOTTOM *Karin Lichey vaults the University of Georgia to an NCAA championship.* (SEE PAGE 130)

TOP *Maureen "Little Mo" Connolly wins nine Grand Slam titles in four years.* (SEE PAGE 168)

BOTTOM *Nancy Lopez brightens every golf tournament with a smile.* (SEE PAGE 170)

Peggy Fleming captivates the world with her grace and style. (SEE PAGE 102)

BACK-UP CRIMSON GOALIE SAVES TITLE

"Come now, let us reason together," says the Lord. "Though your sins are like scarlet, they shall be as white as snow; though they are red as crimson, they shall be like wool. If you are willing and obedient, you will eat the best from the land." —ISAIAH 1:18-19

A back-up freshman goalie rarely sees much action in postseason play. But when Harvard's Allison Kuusisto received the call for the 1999 Women's College Hockey National Championship game, she stepped into the crease and performed like a veteran.

In the semifinals, the Harvard Crimson led Brown, 5–3, with just over 3 minutes left in the game. Harvard played defensively, trying to run out the clock.

As the Bears desperately fought to close the 2-goal gap, a Brown defender slammed into Harvard goalie Crystal Springer. The blow shattered Springer's collarbone, breaking it for the second time that season.

The Crimson called upon Allison Kuusisto to defend the net for the first time in the playoffs. Fortunately, she had gained valuable experience starting nine earlier games while Springer recovered from her first injury.

Harvard faced a powerful University of New Hampshire team in the finals. The Wildcats sought revenge after losing in overtime, 5–4, to the Crimson in the Eastern Collegiate Athletic Conference championship.

The contest matching the nation's top two offensive teams featured 5 ties and 5 lead changes. Sophomore winger Angie Francisco scored twice in the third period to give the Crimson a 5–3 lead, but goals by New Hampshire's Carisa Zaban and Samantha Holmes sent the game into overtime.

Francisco drew a 2-minute penalty for high sticking less than 2 minutes into the extra period. New Hampshire, who had twice capitalized on power plays in regulation, skated fiercely for the win over the depleted Harvard squad.

But Kuusisto focused on covering the puck and not allowing rebounds. Four times she blocked shots entering the goal during Francisco's penalty.

After nearly 8 minutes of overtime play, 1998 Olympic gold medalist A.J. Mleczko passed across the crease to freshman Jen Botterill on the right post. The AWCHA Tournament MVP and Ivy League Rookie of the Year slammed the puck high past the Wildcats goaltender into the far corner of the net bringing victory to the Crimson.

Although Jen got the winning goal, Allison saved the game. She proved willing and obedient when the coach called her off the bench. Her outstanding play covered both Crystal's injury and Angie's error to get Harvard through their short-skate. Together the Crimson became the best in the land.

In the Bible, the Prophet Isaiah tells of another who saves us from our errors and the injuries caused by our sinful ways. The Lord invites us to reason together with Him. When we go to God in obedience, He washes away our wrongs. Isaiah compares those sins to blotches of scarlet on snow or splatters of crimson on pure, undyed wool. Even using the strongest bleach or lots of sunshine, the spots may fade but never go away.

Yet through God, our stains completely disappear.

Have you ever washed new, red clothes with something white? Especially in hot water, the results are pink. Rose lipstick and cherry-colored candle wax leave their marks on clothes, furniture, or carpets forever. Think about the wonder of God completely washing away your sins. Praise Him for making your life white as snow.

Former Lady Nittany Lion and Mother of Four Returns to Basketball

"What a lioness was your mother among the lions! She lay down among the young lions and reared her cubs."

—EZEKIEL 19:2

Suzie McConnell blistered the basketball court for the Pennsylvania State Lady Nittany Lions in the 1980s. The point guard earned school records for both career steals with 507 and assists at 1,307.

The former Kodak All-American competed in the international arena following her graduation from Penn State in 1988. She and her United States teammates captured gold in the 1988 Seoul (South Korea) Olympic Games and bronze in the 1992 Barcelona (Spain) event.

After her second Olympiad, basketball offered little court time for Suzie. Like many ex-players, she switched to coaching.

The former Penn State star achieved immediate success. She led Oakland Catholic High School to a Pennsylvania State Championship in 1993.

Meanwhile, Suzie married Pete Serio, and the couple started a family. First came Pete, then Jordan, followed by Matt and Madison.

While the twice Olympic guard waited for Madison to arrive, the Women's National Basketball Association (WNBA) began operations. Newspaper and television coverage made Serio anxious to leave the bench and return to the court.

Pete encouraged Suzie's comeback and baby-sat during training sessions. She required months of practice to regain shooting, passing, and dribbling skills.

The Cleveland Rockers signed the 32-year-old point guard. Serio immediately cracked the starting lineup, averaging 8.6 points and 6.4 assists per game. The Rockers won the WNBA's

Eastern Conference Championship but fell in the semifinals to the Phoenix Mercury, two games to one.

Numerous honors came Suzie's way during the off-season. She earned an All-WNBA First Team berth and received both the WNBA's Newcomer of the Year and Sportsmanship awards. *Jane Magazine* named Serio one of the nation's Ten Gutsiest Women of 1988, and *Cleveland Magazine* selected her as one of Cleveland's 50 Most Interesting People.

Suzie McConnell Serio made quite a comeback and quite an impression. Her life would have felt fulfilled with college records, Olympic medals, a husband, four children, and successful coaching. But Suzie willed herself to work for more. She wanted a chance to play professional basketball in the United States—an opportunity not available when she graduated from college.

And Serio did it. Not only did she make the team, she won honors. Her children, her cubs, surely took pride in their Nittany Lion and Rocker mother's accomplishments.

The Bible emphasizes the importance of mothers. Moms listen, support, encourage, discipline, teach, train, and serve as examples for their families. They provide for the physical and emotional needs of their children. Godly mothers set the spiritual tone for the home. They sacrifice themselves and pour their love over the boys and girls God gives them, expecting nothing in return.

The rewards come from the Heavenly Father and in quick hugs and wet kisses.

Write a love note to your own mother or to a Christian mother you admire. Tell her what she means in your life, and let her know how you feel. Praise the Lord for godly mothers.

WILLIAMS PERSISTS TO EARN 100-METER RECORD

> *God "will give to each person according to what he has done." To those who by persistence in doing good seek glory, honor and immortality, he will give eternal life.*
>
> —ROMANS 2:6-7

Angela Williams watched her father run at the track when she was just a child. By age 9, she had embarked on a running career of her own.

The aspiring sprinter joined the Southern California Cheetahs, a junior track club based in Los Angeles. In a very short time, the schoolgirl held the record in her age bracket for every event in which she competed.

The youthful speedster continued her success at Chino High School. As a freshman, Angela won the 400 meters at the 1995 California state track meet. Several months later, she received national acclaim by capturing first in the 100 meters at the Junior Pan Am Games.

A pulled hamstring marred her sophomore season, but the prep athlete captured two state titles, the 100 meters and long jump as a junior. Her senior year, Angela increased the gold medal count to three with victories in the 100, 200, and long jump.

Throughout high school, the fleet teenager flirted with the record book. In 1997, she recorded a 10.98, the first sub-11-second 100 meters ever run by a female high school student. Because of excessive wind, her clocking did not register as an official record. At the 1998 California state meet, Williams ran a 11.10 100 meters, the fastest in high school history, but too much wind nullified the record once more.

In the 1998 U.S. Junior Track and Field Championships, Angela finally achieved her long-sought goal. She blazed down the 100-meter runway in 11.11 seconds, besting Marion Jones' high school mark of 11.15 and Chandra Cheeseborough's national record of 11.13. This time no wind blew to taint her time.

Williams received scholarship offers from every NCAA Division I University in the country. She enrolled at the University of Southern California and competed as a freshman in the 100 meters and the 4 x 10 relay.

Angela worked very hard to capture the record for the 100 meters. Twice officials disallowed her wind-aided time. But she persisted and received glory, gold medals, and her name in the record book.

What she had accomplished gave Angela Williams her choice of college track programs. Imagine being able to attend any major university in the United States on scholarship. What an honor and what a credit to the young woman's persistence! She received her reward.

The writers of both Psalms and Proverbs explained about God's rewards. The Heavenly Father gives according to what each person has done, good or bad. However, the Apostle Paul took their words and added to them. Persistence in seeking God's glory and following His truth results in eternal life.

The opposite holds true as well. Those who persist in doing evil move themselves away from God and eternity with Him.

Think of a sport, skill, task, or activity in your life that needs improvement. You may want to choose spending more time with God in prayer and Bible study. Develop a plan for reaching your objective. Ask God to help you be persistent in accomplishing your goal.

COMETS OVERCOME MERCURY TO CAPTURE WNBA THRONE

To him who overcomes, I will give the right to sit with me on my throne, just as I overcame and sat down with my Father on his throne. —REVELATION 3:21

The Houston Comets won the first Women's National Basketball Association (WNBA) Championship over the New York Liberty in 1997. In the league's second year, the Texas team proved virtually unstoppable, winning 27 games and losing only 3 during the regular season.

The 1998 playoffs didn't alter Houston's invincible image. In the semifinals, the defending champions easily dispatched the Charlotte Sting in 2 games.

The Comets faced the runner-up of their conference, the Phoenix Mercury, in the finals. Most anticipated another 2-game title sweep, but the underdogs had differing ideas.

In game one on the Mercury's homecourt, Phoenix pulled a major upset, defeating the Western Conference champions, 54–51. The series moved to Houston with the Arizona team seeking a road victory and title rings.

The Mercury opened game two with great intensity while the Comets performed as if in a daze. With 7:24 remaining, Phoenix led 62–50, and the majority of watchers believed a new champion would be crowned that night.

Houston coach Van Chancellor made a key substitution. He inserted Janet Arcain for ailing defensive ace Kim Perrot to guard the red hot Michele Timms.

The sharpshooting guard had scored 18 points in the game's first 33 minutes. Arcain held Timms to 3 over the remainder of the contest.

WNBA MVP Cynthia Cooper and Sheryl Swoopes keyed the offensive comeback. In a 13–2 run, Swoopes blocked a shot and set in motion a fast break for a Cooper layup.

Moments later, Sheryl's transition basket following a Cooper feed brought Houston to within one, 62–61. Down the stretch, Cynthia scored the Comets' final 4 points in regulation, sending the game into overtime at 66–all.

Leading 70–69 in the extra period, Swoopes hit an 18-footer from the top of the circle. On the Mercury's next possession, the former Texas Tech All-American grabbed the rebound and passed to Cooper. The League MVP drew the foul and hit two free throws with 11 seconds left to play.

The Comets overcame almost certain defeat and emerged with an incredible 74–69 overtime victory. Two nights later, Houston won 80–71 to retain the WNBA crown.

The Houston Comets rose above the circumstances of the first playoff game and most of the second one. They shook off sloppy and selfish play. They regrouped and took the offensive. They made the most of every opportunity. They earned the right to take the throne.

In the last book in the Bible, Revelation, Christ talked about overcoming circumstances. He promised that if we trust Him to help us rise above the sinfulness and selfishness of the world, we will sit on the throne of heaven with Him.

Trust Him.

Attend a women's basketball game, watch one on television, or shoot a few hoops. Examine what it takes to overcome the competition on the court. Think about conditioning, quickness, practice, coaching, and anticipation of the opponent's moves. Consider what it takes to overcome sin and selfishness in the world. Remember, it's no less difficult than overcoming on the court. Praise God for His throne and for helping you rise above the world.

> *Night and day we pray most earnestly that we may*
> *see you again and supply what is lacking in your faith.*
>
> **—1 THESSALONIANS 3:10**

To show her admiration for outstanding play, Nancy Lopez hugged Alison Nicholas at the completion of the third round of the 1997 United States Women's Open golf tournament. Although the 40-year-old LPGA Hall of Famer and four-time Player of the Year had failed in 20 opportunities for the Grand Slam event, overcoming Nicholas' 3-stroke lead appeared possible even if unlikely.

But Lopez, a Roswell, New Mexico, native had carded three rounds in the 60s for a three-day total of 206. Another sub-70 outing might position the veteran golfer for victory.

Nancy began the final day at a torrid pace, sinking birdies on three of the first four holes. But Alison matched her stroke-for-stroke and went one better, chipping off the number four green for an eagle.

The 5-foot tall Englishwoman remained in command until the 14th hole. A double-bogey cut her margin to a single stroke. But the challenger failed to capitalize on the leader's mistakes. Lopez bogeyed 15 and 17 and stepped to the last tee box down 1.

Both golfers hit drives that landed within 3 feet of each other in the fairway. Nancy put her second shot short and to the right of the green. She chipped, placing the ball 15 feet behind the cup.

Meanwhile Nicholas reached the green in 3 and putted from 18 feet away. Her ball stopped inches from the hole.

Lopez lined up her birdie putt to tie and force a playoff. But her stroke pushed the ball just to the right. It slid past the hole, insuring Nancy's fourth U.S. Women's Open runner-up finish and 21st appearance without an Open triumph.

The 35-year-old Nicholas tapped in and emerged victorious

with a 274, 10-under-par total. Lopez tallied a 69 for a four-day score of 275. She became the only player in LPGA history to record four U.S. Open rounds in the '60s and fail to finish in first place.

Nancy Lopez earnestly desired to win the United States Open championship. Year after year she worked toward her goal. Year after year for 21 years, she didn't win. Four times she almost made it, but not quite. She even played brilliantly, carding a score that would have won any previous Open. But it still didn't happen.

What was lacking—focus, practice, confidence? Had she known, she would have supplied the missing element.

Sometimes it's hard to see clearly what we lack, particularly in our relationship with God. The Father gives some of His followers the ability to understand what other Christians need in their lives. Then together, they can work to supply those needs no matter what they might be—faith, prayer, Bible study, discipleship, or ministry.

The Apostle Paul had such insight. He shared his advice freely in his biblical letters.

Why do you think Nancy Lopez had trouble winning the U.S. Open golf championship? Discuss your thoughts with a friend. In what spiritual areas do you have difficulty? If you have problems answering, visit with a church leader or other trusted Christian. Work to supply what is lacking. Ask the Lord to guide you.

Graceful Gold-Medal-Winner Helps Rebuild U.S. Figure Skating

I will build you up again and you will be rebuilt, O Virgin Israel. Again you will take up your tambourines and go out to dance with the joyful. —JEREMIAH 31:4

In 1961, Peggy Fleming lost her skating coach, Billy Kipp, in a plane crash that took the lives of eighteen members of the United States figure skating team. The 13-year-old skater dedicated her life to honoring his memory by always performing at her competitive best.

The daughter of a newspaper pressman captured the first of her five consecutive United States National Championships at age 15. Shortly afterward, she earned a spot on the 1964 U.S. Olympic team and placed sixth in the Innsbruck (Austria) games.

In 1966, Peggy won the first of three straight World Championships. Her success on the ice made Fleming a heavy favorite for the gold medal in the 1968 Olympics.

The slender, 105-pound American beauty combined precision with grace. Her compulsory figures rarely deviated from perfection, and her free skate performances enthralled both judges and audiences with beauty and style drawn from Peggy's ballet training.

On February 10, 1968, a worldwide television audience tuned in live and in color to the Grenoble (France) Olympic Games for Fleming's presentation. She had built a 77.2 lead in the school figures, and a solid free skate would clinch the gold medal.

Dressed in a flowing chartreuse chiffon dress, the American floated across the ice to the strains of Tchiakovsky's *Pathetique*. Moments later, the music changed to the melodious Overture from *Romeo and Juliet*. Her act concluded with sounds from Saint-Saen's opera, *Samson and Delilah*.

Every movement fit the mood and the melody. All eyes focused on the ballerina on ice. Experts and spectators alike acclaimed that her grace had taken the sport to new heights.

The judges unanimously agreed. They awarded Peggy Fleming first in the free skate and the gold medal, the solitary one claimed by the United States in the 1968 Winter Olympics.

The 1961 plane crash literally devastated the young girl and figure skating in the United States. The tragic accident claimed most of the country's talent as they traveled to the world championships. Peggy faced recapturing the joy of skating as her new coach, Carlo Fassi, faced rebuilding the American figure skating team.

Fleming became Fassi's and the United States' first Olympic gold medal winner of the refashioned team. She regained her enchanting delight on ice, and the country gained a worthy champion.

God promised the Prophet Jeremiah that He would rebuild His people, and they would once again sing and dance for joy. The Heavenly Father kept His promise when the Israelites returned to the Promised Land from exile in Babylon. They rebuilt Jerusalem and there was much singing and dancing for joy.

Today when difficulty comes and tragedy strikes, God's promises remain secure. He walks with us. He builds us up and helps rebuild our lives. The Lord restores our joy and allows us to sing and dance with delight once more—if we let him.

Listen to the three musical pieces that Peggy Fleming chose for her Olympic free skate. If you don't own the recordings, borrow them from the public library or enjoy them with a friend who loves classical music. Consider the gold medal winner's emotions as she overcame hard times to feel joy. Praise God for His promises to rebuild our lives and restore our joy.

Davenport Wins Respect and Wealth at Wimbledon

A kindhearted woman gains respect, but ruthless men gain only wealth. —PROVERBS 11:16

American Lindsay Davenport faced German Steffi Graf in the 1999 Wimbledon final. The match-up seemed somewhat surprising since Graf battled injuries through the tournament, and Davenport preferred hard courts to England's soft grass. But from the outset, both competitors played almost flawless tennis.

Graf, a five-time Wimbledon champion, served the first game. The contest went to deuce three times before Davenport set up breakpoint with a forehand that clipped the baseline and handcuffed her opponent. The American broke Steffi's serve on the next point, driving a backhand within inches of the sideline out of the German's reach.

From that point on, the match swayed back and forth. Lindsay faced breakpoint in game two but rallied to hold. Taking advantage of her service break in the first game, the Newport Beach, California, resident claimed the first set, 6–4.

Set two followed the same script. Graf pushed Davenport to breakpoint in her first service game, but the 6-foot-2-inch, 22-year-old player countered with a forehand in the corner and refused to yield.

With the score tied 5–5 and Steffi serving, the 30 year old netted a backhand, giving Lindsay the advantage. On breakpoint, Davenport angled a crosscourt forehand winner that Graf barely touched.

The Grand Slam hopeful took a deep breath and prepared to serve for match. Lindsay aced the first point with a 91 MPH shot that tailed away from Steffi.

At 30–15, Davenport rang up another winner with a 95 MPH

precision serve. Two points later, she served up the middle and watched as Graf dumped the return harmlessly into the net.

The American shrieked slightly, shed several tears, then smiled. The two competitors hugged at the net and walked toward the Duchess of Kent for the awards ceremony.

Lindsay, though obviously excited, maintained an air of calm and reserve. Steffi, though obviously disappointed, exhibited no remorse. In her post-match interview, Davenport called Graf, "the greatest player that's ever played."

Although tennis has traditionally been a polite game, filled with respect and good taste, many recent players have given in to belligerent actions, ruthless comments, and poor sportsmanship. But those present at Centre Court, along with the millions watching from around the world by television, saw a superlative match. Lindsay and Steffi both played terrific tennis. Both conducted themselves with grace and poise.

Kindness to each other, to the officials, and to all present captured the respect of the spectators during the match, throughout the trophy presentation, and afterward in the traditional press conference.

The writer of the Bible Book of Proverbs reminds us of the difference between kindness and ruthlessness. Ruthless behavior may result in wealth, but only the material kind. Kindhearted behavior earns respect and yields wealth in friends. And it doesn't eliminate money either. After all, Davenport won $655,200 for her Wimbledon efforts.

Think about the rules and practices that make tennis a gentle and polite game compared to some other sports. If you get stuck, check a rulebook or watch a match. Confess to the Heavenly Father times when you have been ruthless. Ask God to help you be kindhearted like Him.

While he was still speaking, another messenger came and said, "The fire of God fell from the sky and burned up the sheep and the servants, and I am the only one who has escaped to tell you." —JOB 1:16

Cuban officials sent Ana Fidelai Quirot to a special school because they incorrectly diagnosed her as learning disabled. While attending the institution, a track coach discovered Ana racing barefoot and visualized the child's athletic potential.

The young woman developed into one of the world's best middle-distance runners. She won gold medals in both the 400 and 800 meters at the 1987 and 1991 Pan American Games and a bronze in the 1992 Barcelona Olympics 800. *Track and Field News* selected Quirot as their 1989 Female Athlete of the Year.

But in January 1993, a kerosene cooking stove blew up in Ana's apartment. The flames engulfed the upper half of her body, causing third degree burns.

The Cuban runner spent days in intensive care fighting for her life. Several months pregnant at the time of the accident, Quirot miscarried during the hospitalization and treatments. Doctors withheld the information, fearing it would lessen her will to live.

Eventually Ana stabilized and grew stronger. Numerous operations followed to replace the damaged skin. Reconstructive surgery limited her head and arm movements.

But Quirot resolved to run again and began exercising while lying in bed. In September 1993, the determined athlete returned to the track. Each step split and cracked her healing skin. Observers winced as they watched her endure such pain.

By 1995, Ana had regained most of her former mobility, endurance, and speed. At the World Track and Field Championships held that year in Goteborg, Sweden, she captured the 800-meter crown with a 1:56.11.

In 1996, the Atlanta Olympic games extravaganza showcased Quirot's tragic story. Despite the pressure, the 33-year-old runner claimed the 800-meter silver medal in 1:58.11. Russia's Svetlana Masterkova took first place at 1:57.73, but Ana declared that for her, the silver meant as much as the gold.

Ana Fidelai Quirot faced tremendous adversity in her life. Misdiagnosed, she found herself in an institution. Pregnant, she miscarried her dreamed-of baby. Burned, she underwent excruciating treatments and surgery. Recovering, she faced months of painful rehabilitation. Running, she bore scars of her trauma.

But the athlete met the obstacles and challenges. Her strength and fortitude provided the power to live and endure. Just competing in the 1996 Olympics would have been enough to show her true character. But Ana received more.

In the Bible, Job faced tremendous adversity in his life. He lost his wealth and his children. He endured painful sores from the soles of his feet to the top of his head. His wife thought he would be better off dead. His friends didn't understand.

But Job met the obstacles and challenges. His faith provided the power to live and praise God. Rebuilding his life would have been enough to show his true character. But the Heavenly Father gave him more. Job 42:10-17 lists His many gifts.

Check your smoke alarm. Change batteries if necessary. Make sure you know what to do in case of fire. Determine the best route out of your home and plan in advance a location to meet family members. Pay attention to exits in hotels and other buildings. Remember, getting out is more important than getting things out. Ask God to keep you safe. Thank Him for the power to overcome adversity.

The end of a matter is better than its beginning, and patience is better than pride. —ECCLESIASTES 7:8

Juli Inkster burst on the Ladies Professional Golf Association (LPGA) tour in a blaze of excitement in 1984. The three-time U.S. Amateur Champion captured two Grand Slam events, the Nabisco Dinah Shore and the du Maurier Classic.

After her extraordinary rookie year, Inkster's career floundered. Except for a Dinah Shore victory in 1989, the California native failed to win another Grand Slam tournament for fifteen years. In 1994, the 39-year-old golfer considered retiring and devoting her energies to her husband and two daughters.

Suddenly, her game returned. In early June of 1999, Juli won her third of the four Grand Slam events, the United States Women's Open. Only a victory in the LPGA Championship remained to complete the sweep.

After three rounds in the 1999 LPGA, Inkster, Nancy Scranton, and Cristie Kerr remained in a three-way tie for the lead at 203. Juli prepared for her final round on Sunday by fixing a breakfast of French toast for her family.

Back-to-back birdies on holes 8 and 9 gave the mother of two a 2-stroke lead heading to the back nine. But Liselotte Neumann and Scranton both pulled into a share of the lead by hole 16.

At that point, Inkster's new found confidence took command. On the final three holes, she carded an eagle and two birdies to tally a 6-under-par 65 for the day. Her four-day total of 268, 16-under-par, bettered Neumann by 4 strokes.

With her victory in the LPGA Open, Juli became only the third female golfer to earn Grand Slam honors. Pat Bradley completed the achievement in 1986, and Mickey Wright captured the triumph in 1962 when the events consisted of the U.S. Open, LPGA, Titleholders, and Western Open.

Juli Inkster's career seemed so promising in the beginning. It appeared she would take on the golfing world and win. Then nothing happened. Rare glimpses of potential disappeared into the also-rans. Yet Juli kept on. Through marriage and births, she stayed on the links.

Finally, after nearly a golfing lifetime and close encounters with quitting, something happened. Inkster found her game and the fame of taking the four titles called the Grand Slam.

What made the difference? Patience—quiet, uncomplaining, endurance under distress. Patience—perseverance and diligence. Patience—tolerant and tender forbearance.

Like Juli Inkster, God wants us to learn patience. It isn't easy in this want-everything-right-now world to be willing to wait without complaint. It isn't easy to persevere quietly or endure without playing a martyr. It isn't easy to be tenderly tolerant.

But with the Heavenly Father's help, we can practice patience. And when we do, the conclusion of a matter will be better than its beginning.

Think of some other models of patience in sports. Golf and figure skating offer many examples. Contemplate some biblical representatives. In Luke 2:25-38, Simeon and Anna showed great endurance in waiting for the birth of Jesus. Is patience a quality you need to work on? Ask God to help you learn patience. Praise the Lord for the perseverance He has with you.

> *But the Lord said to Gideon, "There are still too many men. Take them down to the water, and I will sift them for you there. If I say, 'This one shall go with you,' he shall go; but if I say, 'this one shall not go with you,' he shall not go."*
>
> —JUDGES 7:4

Expectations ran high when the Washington Mystics selected University of Tennessee forward Chamique Holdsclaw as the 1999 top draft pick for the Women's National Basketball Association (WNBA). The two-time collegiate National Player of the Year quickly proved the 1998 League's worst team had made a wise decision.

Media flocked to the MCI Center for Chamique's WNBA debut against the Charlotte Sting. A capacity crowd of 20,674 pumped and stirred the home team's emotions.

The focus of everyone's attention started the game with a flurry. When 1:09 had ticked off the clock, Holdsclaw's fallaway 16-foot jumper from the left wing put the Mystics up 2–0.

Sting defenders dogged the former Tennessee standout at every turn. But she often managed to shoot off her dribble or pass to open teammates. Despite competing against more experienced players, Chamique displayed sufficient flashes of brilliance to justify her number one status.

With 9:16 remaining and the score tied at 63–63, Charlotte switched to a zone defense, forcing Washington to shoot from the outside. The Sting went on an 18–4 run and handed the Mystics an 83–73 loss. Chamique finished her initial contest with 18 points and 6 rebounds.

As the 1999 WNBA season moved along, Holdsclaw improved with each outing. At the mid-season break, the 6-foot-2-inch rookie ranked in the top 20 in nine statistical categories, including fifth in points per game (17.9) and third in rebounding (8.6).

Fans responded to the rising star by placing her in the All-Star game's starting lineup. Rival players began complaining about Chamique's press coverage, a sure sign of her superstar status.

The Washington Mystics had a personnel choice to make. As 1998's bottom team, they had 1999's top pick. From among all the women basketball players coming out of college, they had to select one. They needed to narrow the options and opt for the best.

Surely Mystic management considered height, quickness, shooting accuracy, rebounding ability, and court sense. They probably weighed unselfishness and team spirit. Perhaps they contemplated durability and previous injuries.

They made their decision. And it wasn't long before Chamique Holdsclaw proved them right.

In the Bible Book of Judges, Gideon had a personnel decision to make. About 32,000 men volunteered to fight the Midianites. That was too many. God told his leader to send home all those who were afraid, so 22,000 left. But the 10,000 remaining were still too many.

God told Gideon to sift out the rest by how they drank from the spring. Those who cupped the water in their hands and lapped with their tongues while their eyes watched for enemies stayed. The general sent home the ones who fell to their knees and put their mouths in the stream. The 300 remaining best defeated Midian.

God guides us in making decisions just as He led Gideon. The Lord gives ideas, thoughts, criteria, and commonsense so that we can opt for His best in every choice.

If you had been Mystics management, would you have drafted Chamique Holdsclaw? Why or why not? Think of some decisions you have made recently. What criteria did you use? Did you choose wisely? Thank God for help in making right choices.

EVELYN ASHFORD'S DREAMS COME TRUE

Then the king asked, "What is it, Queen Esther? What is your request? Even up to half the kingdom, it will be given you." —ESTHER 5:3

Evelyn Ashford received a taste of success at the 1976 Montreal Olympics. The virtually unknown 19 year old placed a surprising fifth in the 100 meters.

The daughter of an Air Force sergeant returned to California and began training in earnest for the 1980 Moscow games. At the 1979 Montreal World Games, Evelyn stunned track fans by defeating East Germany's Marlies Gohr.

A few months later, however, the sprinter received disturbing news. President Jimmy Carter ordered an American boycott of the 1980 Summer Olympics to protest the Soviet invasion of Afghanistan.

Evelyn felt devastated and considered quitting her running regime. But dreams of world records and gold medals renewed her resolve.

Ashford enrolled in college and continued to improve. By 1983, every international meet featured fierce competition between her and Gohr. ·

The 27 year old's adopted city of Los Angeles hosted the 1984 summer games. Evelyn qualified for the 100, 200, and 4 x 100 relay, but the threat of a hamstring injury forced her to withdraw from the 200-meter event.

Running carefully, the American sprinter survived three 100-meter preliminary heats. In the finals, she took command at the midway point and blew away the competition, setting an Olympic record of 10.97.

Her victory brought little satisfaction, however, since Gohr did not compete due to an East German Olympic boycott. But the two faced off three weeks later at a meet in Zurich, Switzerland.

Ashford overcame her opponent's fast start and surged to a world record of 10.76 seconds. When the time was made official, Gohr and her East German teammate Ingrid Auerswald stood on either side and raised Evelyn's hands in triumph.

Evelyn Ashford visited the track day after day. Her cleats tore through mile after mile after mile of turf in search of her dream, outrunning Marlies Gohr to win Olympic gold. But just when Ashford pulled close enough to reach her goal, politics intervened. The dream faded.

Evelyn could have given up. She might have retired from the track world and moved on with her life. But she chose to continue, to try once again for Olympic glory in besting Gohr. But once again, politics intervened. She had a chance to make her dream come true in halves, first taking Olympic gold and then outdistancing the East German.

Half of her goal wasn't what she wanted, but half was enough at a time. And eventually, Evelyn Ashford's whole dream came true and more. She stood atop the winner's stand in Los Angeles. Later she topped the podium with Marlies on a lower step. And she captured the world record.

In the Bible, King Xerxes considered half to be more than enough. Twice he offered Queen Esther up to half his kingdom. But the Queen wanted more. She wanted her whole request. She wanted the king to save her people.

And her dream came true and more. She received protection for her people and her enemy's estate. God's children triumphed, and Esther's victory is still celebrated today in the Jewish feast of Purim.

Read the story of Esther in the Bible. Ask God to help you know when to be satisfied with half of your dreams and when to pursue them all.

Olympic Skier Makes Up for Cautious First Run

And they did not do as we expected, but they gave themselves first to the Lord and then to us in keeping with God's will. —2 Corinthians 8:5

Skiing came naturally to Gretchen Fraser. She took up the sport at age 16 and at 21 earned a spot on the 1940 U.S. Olympic ski squad.

But when World War II cancelled the 1940 games, Gretchen put aside her hopes for international competition. Eight long years of waiting finally brought the American skier the first opportunity to showcase her skill.

At the 1948 St. Moritz (Switzerland) Games, the foreign press billed Fraser as "an unknown from America." Fans quickly flocked to her, however, when she captured a silver medal in the later discontinued combined Alpine race.

Gretchen's next opportunity came in the slalom. Unfortun-ately, she drew the number one position out of 31 entrants.

By going first, the American skier faced the treacherous Mount Piz-Nair course without the benefit of anyone's previous experi-ence. She played the role of the guinea pig, discovering the hid-den bumps in the snow, patches of ice, and other variations in the mountain's surface.

As Fraser bolted from the gate, she combined speed with cau-tion. Too much hesitation would cost valuable time. Too much haste would wipe out her chances for a medal.

Gretchen skied the course flawlessly in less than a minute. But the seconds added by her evaluation of the mountain reduced the likelihood of medaling.

Fortunately, the event requires two runs with the combined time determining the winner. Using her knowledge from the ini-tial downhill trip, Gretchen threw caution to the wind the second time around.

She zigged and zagged on the slope with abandon, swiveling through the gates with blazing speed. Fraser completed the course perfectly and captured America's first Alpine gold medal in a time of 1:57.2. Antoinette Meyer of Switzerland took silver at 1:57.5.

Gretchen Fraser accomplished the unexpected. Written off by the press as not a medal contender, the patient skier carried home silver and gold.

Her first run in the slalom combined care and carelessness. She tried to strike a balance between caution and unrestraint. But that second time, she gave herself completely to the mountain in keeping with her will to win.

Too often we do the expected. We move through life with care and caution, making it easy for friends or mere acquaintances to predict our actions.

But God asks that we do the unexpected, that we take risks. Saint Paul writes about unanticipated actions. He tells about the churches in Macedonia. Paul didn't expect sharing. They had little to share. Paul didn't expect generosity. They lived in poverty. He didn't expect service. They needed ministry.

Instead, the Macedonian Christians did the unexpected. They ignored their own needs and gave themselves first to God and then to others.

What do people expect of you? Answer the question in relation to athletics, your home and family, and your Christian life. What wonderful actions could you take first for God and then for others? Ask the Lord to help you.

SMALL SOVIET ACCOMPLISHES SPORT DIPLOMACY

"But you, Bethlehem Ephrathah, though you are small among the clans of Judah, out of you will come for me one who will be ruler over Israel, whose origins are from of old, from ancient times." —MICAH 5:2

Olga Korbut stood only 4 feet, 10 inches tall and weighed 85 pounds. But in 1972, the diminutive Soviet gymnast reigned as a giant in the Olympic world.

The native of Grodno in the Belorussian Republic attended a special gymnastics school headed by Renald Knysh. The Russian coach believed every movement performed on the exercise mat could be replicated on the parallel bars, balance beam, and vaulting horse. He invented safety devices to protect his students and eliminate their fears.

In the 1972 Munich (Germany) games, spectators first witnessed the results of Knysh's incredible training. On the first night of competition while leading the Russians to the team gold, the 17-year-old Korbut executed a half-backward somersault off the high bar and caught the lower one on the way down. She called the move a "flik flak" while viewers gasped in amazement.

Olga's brilliant techniques alone could have won the hearts of millions. But combined with her dancing pigtails and impish smile, she immediately became the world's sweetheart.

After two days of competition, the unthinkable occurred. While performing a relatively simple movement, Korbut fell from the bars. When the judges announced her score of 7.5, the Soviet gymnast burst into tears. A worldwide audience wept with her.

The next day Olga returned to competition as if nothing had happened. She performed with the same enthusiasm and flawless style. At the conclusion of the 1972 games, Korbut had captured individual gold medals in the balance beam and floor exercise and silver on the uneven bars.

At a White House meeting, President Richard Nixon told the tiny Russian she had done more to ease global tensions than the diplomatic corps had accomplished in five years. Bob Hope remarked as he presented her the Gillette Cavalcade of Sports Award, "The world of sports can be a continuing key to improving international relations."

The pixie-sized gymnast flew through the air like the imaginary Peter Pan. And like the storybook character, she captured the hearts of Olympic fans throughout the world.

The United States might have been experiencing Cold War with the Soviets, but Korbut seemed neither cold nor threatening. Olga made the Russian people warm and real. The small teen helped begin the long, slow thawing process between the two powerful nations.

The Prophet Micah wrote of a small village that also impacted the world. He predicted that from the tiny town of Bethlehem, a ruler would come. That ruler would change the world and capture the hearts of people everywhere. That ruler was Jesus.

Jesus did change the world. He captured the hearts of all who would really listen. And He still does.

Think of small-sized people and things that have changed the world. Your list might include such items as the microchip and light bulb and such people as Napoleon and Queen Victoria. Thank God for the tiny baby Jesus born in little Bethlehem town.

Ann Meyers Attempts to Follow Brother's Example

To this you were called, because Christ suffered for you, leaving you an example, that you should follow in his steps.
—1 PETER 2:21

Sam Nassi, owner of the NBA's Indiana Pacers, signed former UCLA collegiate basketball star Ann Meyers to a $50,000 free agent contract in September 1979. Most believed Nassi signed the 24-year-old four-time All-American as a publicity stunt.

But Ann refused to be a part of any silly promotion. The 1978 College Player of the Year considered the offer a legitimate opportunity to play in the NBA and was determined to make the most of it.

In the weeks prior to free agent camp, the 1976 Olympic team member worked out with her brothers Jeff and Dave, a forward with the Milwaukee Bucks. When camp opened at Butler University's Hinkle Field House, she had never been more prepared both physically and mentally to play basketball.

Ann performed adequately in practice, but attitudes needed adjustment. Pacer coach Bob "Slick" Leonard attempted to talk the former UCLA Bruin out of her tryout. Two-year veteran player John Kuester knocked Meyers to the floor in a scrimmage, but she acted as if nothing happened.

Reporters' silly questions bothered the NBA hopeful most. Many appeared more concerned about shower and dressing room facilities than Ann's passing, shooting, and ball-handling abilities.

After six practice sessions in three days, Leonard took the future NBC commentator aside for a private conversation. Although he hemmed and hawed about her release, the message came through loud and clear. The coach had acquiesced to the owner's wishes and let her try out, but in his opinion, the tryout had ended.

Based on her performance compared to the other free agents,

Ann believed the Pacers should have taken her to training camp with the veterans. But at the time, the idea that a woman could play basketball with men seemed incomprehensible to them.

To minimize the sideshow feeling, Meyers rejected book and commercial offers focusing on her experience. She remained grateful that for at least three days she had felt like a basketball player without reference to her gender.

Imagine Ann's excitement when she received the call to sign with the Indiana Pacers. The $50,000 added credibility to the offer. Having grown up playing basketball with guys bolstered her confidence. Meyers wanted to emulate her brother's example and follow his footsteps in the NBA. She knew she could do it.

But she couldn't—not because of her ability, but because of perceptions. They focused on the peripheral instead of the important. And she suffered.

In life, we choose people to emulate. We find the footsteps we want to follow. Sometimes our selections work. Occasionally we discover our ideal disappoints us, and we change directions. At other times, as in Ann's case, circumstances prevent us from reaching our goal.

Yet there's one example who will never disappoint us. His footsteps remain steady. His path always leads in the right direction. Circumstances won't intervene. The only way we won't reach our goal of living like Him is if we fail. He won't.

That perfect one is Jesus Christ who suffered for us.

Who do you look up to? In whose footsteps do you try to follow? Is it a family member, friend, teacher, Christian leader, or simply someone you admire from afar? Remember another person may have already chosen you as their ideal. Ask God to guide you to select worthy earthly examples and to help you follow in Christ's footsteps as a godly model for others.

"THE ROCK" SAVES THE GAME

My God is my rock, in whom I take refuge, my shield and the horn of my salvation. He is my stronghold, my refuge and my savior. —2 SAMUEL 22:3

Briana Scurry's teammates dubbed her "The Rock" and "The Wall" for her outstanding defensive play. But after their semifinal match against Brazil in the 1999 Women's World Cup (WWC), they switched to calling her "The Savior" instead.

Palo Alto's Stanford Stadium hosted the prelude to the WWC final on the Fourth of July. More than 73,000 fans celebrated Independence Day by witnessing these superstars in their quest for world soccer supremacy.

Unlike the earlier elimination matches, the United States played strong defense from the outset. In the game's fifth minute, the Americans received a huge offensive break.

Julie Foudy sent a long cross kick from the right wing that appeared to be headed straight for the Brazilian goalie's hands. As Maravilha leaped, however, the ball caromed off her fingertips, and Cindy Parlow butted it forcefully into the net for a U.S. goal.

The United States pressed offensively for a while before Brazil began to click with their passes. Scurry's diving hand knocked away Pretinha's shot in minute 30, and Michelle Akers cleared the ball near the goal on her cross kick moments later. The first half ended with the Americans leading, 1–0.

After intermission, the U.S. goalkeeper turned from superb to sensational. Scurry first tipped Nene's 35-foot shot over the net, and minutes later her hand grazed the Brazilian's kick just enough to send it wide.

Brazil lobbed the ball clear and to the right side in the contest's 60th minute, but the former University of Massachusetts player sprinted and knocked the ball out of play before Sissi could reach it. Scurry then smothered the ensuing corner kick before the opposition could set a play.

In minute 80, the United States gained some breathing room on Akers' penalty kick goal. Three minutes later, the American goalkeeper quashed her opponent's dying hopes with a sprawling two-handed stop on Pretinha.

Following their 2–0 victory, the United States team rushed to the far end of the field to congratulate their goalie on the 52nd shutout of her career. Tournament officials wisely awarded Scurry the game's Most Valuable Player honors.

Each time the Brazilians sent the ball into the net, it hit a boulder. That rock took the form of the goalie. Briana Scurry was indeed the rock of the American team. She shielded her squad from opponents' scores and saved them from defeat. Briana provided confidence for her teammates and handed them the opportunity to win.

Young King David found his rock in God. God delivered him from the Philistines and from Saul. The Lord shielded David from his enemies and saved him from harm from wild animals. Yahweh lifted him with confidence, and the king relied on his Heavenly Father for strength and purpose.

In the days since David lived, God's strength hasn't weakened. His refuge remains safe. His salvation stays sure. The Lord is our rock and our salvation now and forevermore. Amen.

Try to dig up a large rock. Could you do it? If you could, how hard would you have to work? Push against a stone wall or large boulder. Did you move it? Praise the Rock of your Salvation. Thank the Lord for the refuge He gives.

DIZZINESS ALMOST DOWNS DIVER

> *But the Pharisees and the teachers of the law who*
> *belonged to their sect complained to his disciples,*
> *"Why do you eat and drink with tax collectors and 'sinners'?"*
> *Jesus answered them, "It is not the healthy who need a doctor,*
> *but the sick." —LUKE 5:30-31*

Mary Ellen Clark, the youngest of seven children, began diving at age 7. Her father, Gene, a former University of Pennsylvania diving team captain, served as her first coach.

After four years of competition and graduating from Pennsylvania State University in 1986, the 5-foot, 1-inch diver completed a master's in physical education at Ohio State in 1989. To support her continuing diving efforts, she worked at several odd jobs, including selling knives.

At the 1992 Olympic diving trials, Mary Ellen stunned the field by claiming the second slot on the team on her final attempt. She amazed the entire world at the Barcelona (Spain) games with a bronze medal. At age 29, the former Penn State athlete became the oldest Olympic diving medalist.

But in 1995, Clark's career almost ended. She suffered from vertigo, a feeling of dizziness, an impossible condition for a diver leaping from a 3-meter platform.

Mary Ellen tried numerous remedies including acupuncture, sleeping upright, and vitamin and herbal therapy. She finally achieved relief through chiropractic manipulation and massage.

At the 1996 Olympic trials, the Barcelona bronze medalist trailed Becky Ruehl and Eileen Richetelli after three of five dives. But Richetelli badly botched her fourth attempt and fell to third while Clark vaulted into first.

Two weeks later in the Atlanta games, the American ranked ninth following the semifinals. Clark moved into third after two

of the final five dives but fell to sixth with a poor effort on number three.

But the Pennsylvania native rallied on the last two dives and regained her third spot for her second Olympic bronze. She extended by four years her record as the Olympic's oldest diving medalist. China's Fu Mingxia won the gold, and Germany's Annika Walter took the silver.

Sometimes children turn round and round until they're too dizzy to stand up. Others play swinging statue, the game in which one person twirls another around and around, flinging him or her to fly into a "frozen" position. Seeing the world whirl can be fun for a moment, but not for long.

For Mary Ellen Clark, that dizzy feeling of vertigo could have led to serious injury with a fall from the diving platform onto concrete or the side of the pool. More than 10 feet is a long way to plunge.

The Olympic diver tried lots of remedies, some traditional and some not so traditional. Fortunately, Clark finally went to the right doctor for her and found a cure.

One of the many names for Jesus is the Great Physician. Not only did Jesus heal broken bodies, he also healed broken spirits.

When we have physical problems, we sometimes try home remedies or put off going to the doctor. Likewise, when we have spiritual needs, we attempt to treat ourselves with self-help books and homemade cure-alls. What we really need is to go to the Great Physician through prayer, Bible study, and worship.

Read the account of Jesus healing the paralytic in Luke 5:17-26. Thank Him for the miracles of healing in the Bible and for His gifts of skilled doctors and modern medicine. Praise the Great Physician for spiritual healing.

"Wisdom is with aged men, with long life is understanding." —JOB 12:12

Driving from her home in Lexington, Kentucky, to Columbus, Ohio, for a tryout with the American Basketball League's (ABL) Quest, Valerie Still stopped at the mall. After two years in retirement from the Italian professional leagues, she didn't own a pair of basketball shoes.

Many advised the two-time University of Kentucky All-American that she couldn't perform up to ABL standards. But Valerie never listened to negative comments.

After leading Como to an Italian title in 1991, a serious automobile accident threatened Still's life. A speeding car cut in front of Valerie, and she drove into a tree. The league superstar suffered a shattered pelvis, broken wrist, severe facial lacerations, and a fractured vertebrae.

Doctors feared Valerie might never walk again, but within months, Kentucky's all-time leading scorer with 2,763 points returned to the court. She played four more seasons overseas before returning to the United States.

Although many American athletes experienced frustration playing in Europe, the 6-foot, 1-inch center relished living abroad. She became fluent in Italian and hosted her own television show.

The European leagues also brought Still and her husband Rob together. He played basketball at Kentucky, but the pair never met in college because they attended UK at different times.

The Quest signed the 35-year-old center to add maturity and experience to its young roster. In the ABL's inaugural 1996–97 season, Columbus reached the championship finals against the Richmond Rage.

After falling behind 2–1 in the best-of-five series, the Quest claimed back-to-back wins to capture the initial league title.

Valerie captured the championship MVP trophy, averaging 14.2 points per game over the five contests.

The following year, Columbus paced the ABL with a 36–8 record and faced the Long Beach Stingrays in the finals. The Quest lost the first two meetings but rallied to win three in a row for its second straight title. Still reclaimed the MVP award, scoring 25 points in the championship game.

Two MVP trophies! What an accomplishment for a mid-thirties athlete who had overcome potentially paralyzing injuries. Most didn't believe Valerie could make the team. Then when she did, they didn't think she would start. After that, they wouldn't view her as a star.

But they were wrong. Age had its place. Still had her skills, and she had more. She had wisdom, maturity, and experience.

In today's youth-oriented society, many don't believe older folks have much value. And when they find a niche, most don't think it's very important. But they are wrong. Age has its place. Older people possess skills and more. They add wisdom, maturity, and experience.

God knows that, and so should we.

List some famous people who made their greatest contributions late in life. Choose modern day persons as well as those who lived in Bible times. Get to know some older people who live near you. Seek their advice and counsel. Praise God for the wisdom and experience older people bring to your church and community.

ANKLE INJURES THOMAS' PERFORMANCE

From him the whole body, joined and held together by every supporting ligament, grows and builds itself up in love, as each part does its work. —EPHESIANS 4:16

Debi Thomas fell in love with figure skating while watching a live performance of the Ice Follies. At age 7, she practiced her skating lessons six hours a day and enjoyed every moment in the rink. The young girl described the sensation on the ice as "walking without moving."

Her divorced mother often scrimped on necessities and sacrificed time and energy to support her daughter's dreams. The programmer/analyst in California's Silicon Valley sewed costumes, beaded the dresses, choreographed routines, repaired broken skates, and chauffeured Debi between school, practice, and competition.

Judges eventually took notice of the San Jose, California native's natural athleticism. In 1985, the U.S. Olympic Committee selected Thomas as the Amateur Athlete of the Year.

The following season brought greater success and acclaim. Debi captured the United States Figure Skating gold and wrestled the world championship from two-time defending title holder Katarina Witt.

But an Achilles tendon injury suffered in 1987 reduced the 20-year-old skater's jumping ability, and she lost her American title to Jill Trenary. Thomas turned to ballet lessons to improve her form. She trained under the world-renowned Mikhail Baryshnikov and regained the U.S. championship in 1988.

The Calgary (Canada) Winter Olympics and Debi's gold medal dream awaited, but the effects of the injury remained. Determined to show the world her athleticism, the 5-foot, 6-inch skater attempted to jump higher, more often, and with greater difficulty.

She succeeded in the leaps, but her bad ankle caused several shaky landings. Debi settled for the bronze while Witt captured her second gold, and Canada's Elizabeth Manley took silver on her home ice.

Following a third place finish in the 1988 World Championships, Thomas retired from amateur competition. She performed briefly professionally but primarily concentrated on her studies. In 1997, the two-time United States champion graduated from Northwestern University's Medical School.

Without the ankle injury, perhaps Debi Thomas could have captured another women's figures skating Olympic gold medal for the United States. But that one tiny tendon created time off the ice. That small part of the body caused shaky landings and insecurity.

The invisible connective tissue failed in its purpose. The sinew didn't do its job, preventing Debi's whole body from reaching its potential. And the skater chose to devote her life to healing the human body.

Paul called the church the body of Christ. Just as in the human form, each part has a special and important role, so in the church each person has a place to fill. It might be as an apostle, pastor, teacher, prophet, evangelist, encourager, greeter, musician, or administrator.

But no matter how invisible or in the background the responsibility may be, each part must work in concert and in love. Only then can the church be the body of Christ as God intends.

What role do you play in your church? Have you discovered your gifts? If you haven't yet found where God wants you to serve, ask Him to guide you into the place He has chosen for you. Thank the Lord for His church.

SLIPPING SHOE MAKES FOR TIGHT RACE

Stand firm then, with the belt of truth buckled around your waist, with the breastplate of righteousness in place, and with your feet fitted with the readiness that comes from the gospel of peace. —EPHESIANS 6:14-15

Losing a shoe never occurred to Leigh Daniel. But in a tight race anything can happen, and the runner must be ready.

Observers favored the Texas Tech University distance runner in the 10,000 meters at the 1999 NCAA Track and Field Championship based on her personal best of 32:53.95. However when the gun sounded, an extremely cautious field packed the competitors together like sardines.

About a kilometer into the race, a contestant caught Leigh's heel, and her shoe slipped off. She shuffled along for a lap and a half before catching the voice of track coach David Smith. He yelled for her to stop and fix the loose footwear.

Since the young woman double-knots her laces, Daniel halted, bent over, untied the two knots, slipped her shoe back on, and retied the laces. The procedure seemed to take forever, and the young woman who began running as a high school senior trailed the leaders by 200 meters.

The distance runner recalled a similar situation at Stanford. In that race, the leader broke far in front, but Leigh eventually caught her and recorded the best time of her career.

The unexpected event excited the crowd watching the long and sometimes boring race. They focused on the trailing runner in red and cheered her comeback efforts.

Daniel patiently closed the gap, first passing the stragglers. She reached the back of the pack at the halfway point. Jostled and pushed, Daniel struggled once more for position but managed to avoid serious contact. She moved into the number two slot behind Notre Dame's JoAnna Deeter at the 6K mark.

Deeter tried to widen her lead, but Daniel and Brigham Young's Tara Rohatinsky followed. With two laps remaining, Leigh bolted to the front. She sprinted the final lap in 72.6 and clipped Rohatinsky for first place, winning by less than three seconds in a time of 34:01.63.

The crowd roared. In 30 minutes, Leigh Daniel had gone from favorite to underdog and the fans' darling. Spectators agonized as they watched her replace her shoe. Then they rooted for her comeback. Finally tied back into her cleats, Leigh firmly took the track armed with the truth that she had come from behind before and the peace that she could still win. And win she did.

As Christians we face opposition in life. Some people shun us because of our faith. Others ridicule us for right living. Many attack our ethics or tempt us to do something a little bit wrong. Still more tell us no one will ever know if we stray from God's path.

Paul warned the Ephesians to stand firm. He likened the struggle to battle and reminded Christ's followers of the armor provided. The apostle urged them to buckle on the belt of truth, to put on the breastplate of righteousness, and to tie on the shoes of the gospel of peace.

God makes that same armor available to us today. Those gifts are as important to us as shoes are to distance runners. We must simply remember to wear them.

Count the pairs of shoes in your closet. If you're an athlete, you may own running shoes, cross trainers, cleats, and high tops. You choose based on your activity. Think about how the pieces of the armor of God are also fitted to different tasks. How can you use them to help you in your spiritual growth?

Praise the Lord, O my soul. O Lord my God, you are very great; you are clothed with splendor and majesty. He wraps himself in light as with a garment; he stretches out the heavens like a tent and lays the beams of his upper chambers on their waters. He makes the clouds his chariot and rides on the wings of the wind. —PSALM 104:1-3

The University of Georgia gymnastics team defended their national title at the 1999 NCAA meet at the University of Utah's Huntsman Center. The "Gym Dogs" carried a perfect 31–0 season record into the competition and stood 66–0 following the 1997 NCAA championships.

In collegiate competition, four events—vault, uneven bars, balance beam, and floor exercises —occur over six rotations. A random draw determines the teams' order of participation.

Georgia drew the vault in the first round. The Bulldogs scored the highest total, 49.4, of any team. Senior Karin Lichey led the way with a 9.95 followed by her sophomore sister Kristi at 9.90.

The defending champions enjoyed a second round bye and moved to the uneven bars in the third rotation. Karin, the 1999 SEC Athlete of the Year, paced the squad once more, carding a 9.95. Brooke Anderson followed at 9.80 as the Gym Dogs totaled 49.275.

After the bars, the Bulldogs performed on the beam. In this event, Karin unexpectedly fell from the apparatus and recorded a sub-par 9.40. But Amanda Curry, Emily Chell, and Stacey Galloway topped the squad at 9.875. Kristi Lichey added a 9.85, and Jenni Beathard rounded out with a 9.80, totaling 49.275.

With a second bye in round five, Georgia entered the floor exercises needing a 48.375 to surpass the University of Alabama which had concluded the competition at 195.950. The Bulldogs' first performer, Caroline Harris, stepped out-of-bounds, reducing

her score to 9.50 and leaving no room for another error.

But Karin at 9.95, Kristi with 9.85, Stacey earning 9.85, Suzanne Sears for 9.825, and Jenni getting 9.775 combined for a 49.25 to bring Georgia a repeat triumph with a 196.85 total. The University of Michigan finished runner-up at 196.55, and Alabama claimed third.

The Georgia women stretched to the sky and back down again as they vaulted. They flew on wings of wind through the uneven parallel bars. The Gym Dogs lay their toes and bodies perfectly on the balance beam. The Bulldogs lightly touched the floor exercise mat as they wrapped themselves in tumbles and twirls.

Though clad in Georgia red and white, Karin Lichey and her teammates added the splendor and majesty of gold medals and victory.

The psalmist glorifies God for His splendor and majesty. The Lord stretches out the heavens and wraps the world in light. He sends sunrays from the sky to sparkle on the sea. The Creator clouds the air with lightning and rain while whispering to His children with gentle wind.

Praise the Lord.

Try some floor exercises, including tumbling if you can. Place masking tape on the floor and walk the balance beam. Hang for a few seconds holding to a tree limb. Take a running start as though preparing to vault. Consider the difficulty of the events and the greatness of the gymnasts achievements. Glorify God who made our bodies able to do such amazing feats..

HUTCHERSON FLYING QUEENS SOAR

Does the hawk take flight by your wisdom and spread his wings toward the south? Does the eagle soar at your command and build his nest on high? —JOB 39:26-27

Dr. Bill Marshall, President of Wayland Baptist College, pioneered women's basketball in the late 1940s. His farsighted vision built the small Texas collegiate program into a powerhouse recognized around the world.

Wayland's team played under the regulation of the Amateur Athletic Union (AAU) since no separate organization for women's sports existed at the college level. Harvest Queen, a local grain mill, agreed to provide financial support, and the school adopted the nickname, "Harvest Queens."

Dr. Marshall's long-range plans for the school that later became a university included outreach to international students. He proposed using women's basketball as a goodwill and promotional tool.

In 1948, Wayland scheduled a three-game exhibition series in Mexico City. Managers were unsure about the best transportation venue for the 1,200-mile journey.

Officials discussed the possibility of flying rather than traveling by bus or train. Dr. Marshall contacted an ex-student, Claude Hutcherson, who owned a local flying service, regarding the use of his aircraft.

Hutcherson agreed to underwrite the cost of the trip, and the Queens took their first team flight. The south-of-the-border games drew large crowds, and the excursion enjoyed great success. Hutcherson pledged Dr. Marshall his financial support until another sponsor could be found.

In 1950, the basketball squad came under full sponsorship of Hutcherson Air Service. The school renamed its team, "Hutcherson Flying Queens," in his honor.

During the 1950s and 1960s, the school experienced great court success. Wayland's women won ten AAU championships and finished another ten times as runner-up.

When AAU basketball faded in the late 1960s, the University joined the AIAW and later the NAIA. Through the 1999 season, Wayland Baptist totaled 1,298 victories, the highest of any American women's collegiate program. Hutcherson Air Service continued to sponsor the Flying Queens.

Who would have thought that a famous women's basketball team would be formed in a small town in the Texas panhandle? But Marshall believed it could be done.

He raised money through sponsorships, not the norm for financing collegiate athletics in those days. He recruited outstanding women athletes, and he made them soar in the eyes of the world. His wisdom allowed the Hutcherson Flying Queens to take flight.

But in the natural world, only God can put creatures in the air. Only He can guide the birds to spread their wings and migrate south for the winter and north for the summer. Only the Creator can make the eagle soar to build his aerie, holding delicate eggs and tiny eaglets.

Only the Lord controls the world.

Have fun thinking about possible nicknames for collegiate teams using corporate or business sponsors. Do you suppose any of them would add fame to the university, or do you think the companies would want control for their advertising dollars? Praise God for His control over the world.

There is a time for everything, and a season for every activity under heaven. . . . A time to weep and a time to laugh. —ECCLESIASTES 3:1,4

Andrea Mead's family life revolved around skiing. Her parents operated a ski lodge at Pico Point, Vermont, and at age 4, she took to the slopes.

Ten years later, Andrea qualified for the United States Olympic skiing team at tryouts held in Sun Valley, Idaho. In 1948, at age 15, she traveled to St. Moritz, Switzerland as the youngest American Olympic representative and placed eighth in the slalom.

While competing for her country, the Vermont native met men's team member David Lawrence, a collegiate skier at Dartmouth University. The next year, their relationship blossomed into love after David stumbled at Andrea's feet following a practice run. Her scornful look infuriated Lawrence and spurred him to pursue her.

The couple married in Davos, Switzerland, and both skiers continued their Olympic competition. The 20-year-old Andrea defied tradition by placing enjoyment above winning. David learned to respect his wife's position and told her before each race to have fun rather than wishing her good luck.

In the 1952 Oslo (Norway) games, Mead Lawrence opened in the giant slalom, but poor conditions prevailed. Officials shortened the course to two-thirds of a mile, and 300 Norwegian soldiers shoveled snow from ditches and gullies to cover the bare spots. Despite the hazards, Andrea captured the gold in a time of 2:06.8, bettering Austria's Dagmar Rom by over two seconds.

Three days later in the slalom, the American fell halfway down the course on her first run. Most observers believed making up the lost seconds would be impossible.

With nothing to lose on her second downhill, Mead Lawrence skied with pure joy. She quickly poled through the 49 gates, dar-

ingly crouching low and tightly hugging the mountain. Andrea flew through the finish line into the waiting arms of her husband.

Her incredibly fast second run lowered the combined time to 2:10.6 and edged out Germany's Ossi Reichert for first place. The young woman from Vermont's snowy slopes became America's first double gold Alpine medalist.

Like most newlyweds, Mr. and Mrs. Lawrence found adjustments necessary to form a successful marriage. Today's athletes compete to win because winning means everything in sports. Andrea's philosophy of fun and laughter over victory seemed strange and unusual to her husband.

But adjust they did. David learned not to take the sport quite so seriously and to wish his wife joy. His wife's delight on the snow enabled her to relax and take chances. Ultimately that led to her two gold medals.

Too often in today's world, competition competes with pleasure. Happiness in sport comes not from participating in the activity. Instead, gladness comes only with blue ribbons and gold medals.

But God says there's a time for laughter and enjoyment. While we may weep when we or our favorite team or individual loses, we should delight in participating or in watching athletic contests. We should have fun.

Spend some time enjoying your favorite sport, either as a participant or spectator. Ask yourself if you sometimes take winning too seriously or push so hard the activity is no longer satisfying. Thank God for His gift of sports. Pray that you will always have fun with them.

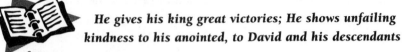

He gives his king great victories; He shows unfailing kindness to his anointed, to David and his descendants forever. —PSALM 18:50

For seven years, Betsy King struggled on the Ladies Professional Golf Association (LPGA) tour. But beginning in 1984, the Furman University graduate reigned supreme.

The Reading, Pennsylvania, native won the 1984 Women's Kemper Open for her first tournament crown. Later that year, she captured the Freedom Orlando Classic and the Columbia Savings Classic, receiving Rolex Player of the Year honors.

Five years later in the 1989 U.S. Women's Open, Betsy experienced an awful third round. The member of the 1976 National Collegiate Championship Team led by as many as 4 strokes but tallied a double-bogey and two bogeys on the last four holes to fall into a tie with Patty Sheehan.

But Patty, frustrated by her triple-bogey on hole 8, carded a 79 in the final round and dropped to a 17th place tie. Meanwhile, King opened with birdies on two of the first three holes and tallied a 68, 3-under-par, for the day. Her four-day 278 total, 6-under-par, bettered Nancy Lopez by 4 strokes.

Coupled with her 1987 Dinah Shore victory, the first place finish brought King her second Grand Slam title. The Open triumph, her fifth of 1989, represented number 19 since 1984. Later in 1989 Betsy captured the Nestle World Championship. The 20 victories made the two-time *Golf Magazine* Player of the Year the winningest golfer over that five-year period.

During the '90s, King continued her outstanding play. Through 1998, she totaled 31 championships including 6 Grand Slams. She repeated as the 1990 Open titlist and claimed 2 more Dinah Shore crowns. In 1995, the LPGA Hall of Fame inducted the 40-year-old golfer, and the following year marked the debut of the

CoreStates Betsy King LPGA Classic.

Betsy King literally became the king of women's golf. She won great victories. But she also showed unfailing kindness in her fame.

Active in LPGA's Christian Fellowship, Betsy gave unselfishly of herself. She organized Habitat for Humanity projects in Charlotte and Phoenix. Two off-seasons saw her accompanying players to work with orphan relief in Romania.

The King of Kings and Lord of Lords gives us great victories in life. They may not be athletic triumphs, but they can be wins over self-doubt, self-consciousness, self-pity, and selfishness. And the Lord shows us kindness. He expects us, like Betsy, to do the same for others.

Try to perform at least one random act of kindness every day. Plan to participate in on-going or one-time ministry projects each year. Watch for opportunities to work with Special Olympics or other athletic events or with Habitat for Humanity. Consider tutoring children or reading to nursing home residents. Deliver Meals on Wheels or collect items for the local pregnancy crisis center or family abuse facility. Do something to share Christ's love with others. Ask God to help you spread His kindness throughout your world.

TENNIS PLAYER CHOOSES DEGREE OVER EARNINGS

Choose my instruction instead of silver, knowledge rather than choice gold, for wisdom is more precious than rubies, and nothing you desire can compare with her.

—PROVERBS 8:10-11

After Duke University junior Vanessa Webb claimed the 1998 NCAA women's singles tennis title, many expected her to turn professional. But the 22-year-old collegiate star preferred academics to the WTA.

The Canadian from Toronto, Ontario, quickly rose to the top of her class. As a freshman, she set a Duke record for wins, finishing her first year at 51–11 and rising to a number seven national rank.

To perfect her game, Webb traveled the professional minor league summer circuit. The collegian won several tournaments, but in order to maintain her NCAA eligibility, refused the prize money.

Vanessa continued this routine throughout her Duke tenure. As a sophomore, she suffered a shoulder injury, cutting her playing time in half. Despite the shortage of matches, the 6-foot left-hander posted a 24–2 mark and climbed to the number-one spot in the collegiate rankings on December 10, 1996.

The graduate of Vaughan Road Collegiate Institute took a high school tennis route different from the norm. Most promising junior players attend tennis academies in Florida, California, or Arizona. Although many programs offered Vanessa a slot, she elected to stay in Toronto with her family and practice indoors much of the year.

In 1998, Webb defeated Stanford's Ania Bleszynski, 6–3, 6–5, in the finals of the NCAA championship, making her the first Duke female tennis player to achieve the honor. The victory secured Webb wild-card invitations to WTA tournaments.

But Vanessa chose to return for her senior year and complete her economics degree. She rejected $75,000 in summer winnings to remain eligible even though her family footed all of her travel bills.

Unfortunately, collegiate tennis' number-one player failed to repeat her title, falling to Georgia's Vanessa Castellano. Webb felt no sorrow for her own defeat but regretted that Duke never won a team title in her four years of competition.

That $75,000 represented a lot of money, but Vanessa Webb knew her priorities. She understood the long-range financial returns of a college degree. She recognized the value of instruction and knowledge. She considered the alternatives and determined to stay in school. Vanessa demonstrated her wisdom in making decisions for the future rather than the present.

Making choices isn't always easy, especially when weighing immediate rewards against long-term gains. But wisdom says we look at all of the options and pick the best. Often that means passing up something we want now in order to get something better later. Athletes who choose to leave college early for professional careers frequently sacrifice tomorrow for today.

The writer of Proverbs tells how God values education, knowledge, and wisdom. He compares them to precious metals and priceless gems. He encourages us to develop our intellects, our knowledge of God's Word, and our good practical judgment so that we may live life the Father's way.

Look in the newspaper, watch a television shopping channel, or visit a jewelry store to determine the value of gold, silver, and rubies. Suppose you were offered the most expensive jewelry you saw in exchange for your knowledge and education. Would it be a tough choice for you? Praise God for His wisdom. Ask Him to help you make wise decisions.

Blue Devils Attack Lady Vols' Strength

A wise man attacks the city of the mighty and pulls down the stronghold in which they trust. —PROVERBS 21:22

The Duke Blue Devils faced a seemingly impossible task—to eliminate the three-time defending national champion Tennessee Lady Vols in the 1999 NCAA Eastern Regional. Despite playing only an hour from the Devils' hometown of Raleigh, the Greensboro, North Carolina, crowd heavily favored number-two-ranked UT. But Duke approached the contest with determination.

Both teams started slowly. Chamique Holdsclaw, the Lady Vols' top scorer and floor leader, missed her first ten shots. Tennessee appeared uninspired and out-of-sync.

Duke, the ACC champion, built intensity and confidence as the contest progressed. Leading 21–18 in the first half, the Blue Devils put together a 12–2 run and led at intermission, 35–24.

Coach Pat Summitt regrouped her team at halftime. Holdsclaw opened the second half with a 3-point play, and her teammates hit 3 more in a row.

Suddenly, Duke's margin narrowed to 38–34. The underdogs continued to play aggressive defense, but their offense sputtered. Toward the middle of the second half, the Blue Devils failed to nail a field goal for over 5 minutes. The lead dropped to one single point, 46–45, with 6:52 remaining.

But the confident, shooting Duke team settled down and slowly began to edge away from the Lady Vols. Nicole Erickson, who had been benched by foul trouble, hit 2 quick baskets to re-energize Duke and put the team in front, 55–50.

The Blue Devils shone at the free-throw line. They sank 12 in the final 1:31 and went 22-of-29 for the game en route to a 69–63 upset.

Chamique Holdsclaw, Tennessee's four-time All-American,

fouled out with 25 seconds remaining, after scoring just 8 points and shooting a mere 2-of-18 from the field. Leaving the contest in tears, she and Coach Summitt embraced for almost a minute before Chamique sat back on the bench with a towel covering her face.

The Duke bench erupted.

Coach Gail Goestenkors had chosen the strategy of containing the mighty Holdsclaw in an effort to win. And it worked. They held the top player in the nation in check and defeated the one-seed in their region. And the Blue Devils had done it in a city partial to the Lady Vols.

For their effort the Eastern College Athletic Conference named the Blue Devils as Division I Women's Basketball Team of the Year after earning its first trip to the NCAA Final Four and championship game. Goestenkors won ACC Coach of the Year honors as well.

In athletics, it's often smart to go after the heart of a team. Pulling down the strong damages the group's trust and creates self-doubts and weakness.

Satan frequently tries the same with us. He goes for our strength, the area we never worry about. Then by tackling our might, he shakes our confidence and fills us with questioning. If we're not careful, he'll damage our faith, our ministry, our worship, our relationships, and our church.

God instructs us to be wise and vigilant. He wants us to trust in Him, not in ourselves. When we live in His strength, we can stand firm against the devil.

Examine the strengths and weaknesses of your favorite basketball team. Put yourself in the place of an opponent. Where would you attack? Examine your own strengths and weaknesses. If you were Satan, where would you assault? Ask God to help you stand strong in Him.

Soccer Program Grows into Champion

Again he said, "What shall we say the kingdom of God is like, or what parable shall we use to describe it? It is like a mustard seed, which is the smallest seed you plant in the ground. Yet when planted, it grows and becomes the largest of all garden plants, with such big branches the birds of the air can perch in its shade." —MARK 4:30-32

The University of North Carolina Tar Heels and the University of Florida Gators met with the 1998 women's NCAA soccer championship on the line. The matchup brought together a long-established program against one barely in its infancy.

The Tar Heels carried a 70-match unbeaten streak and 14 national titles into the contest. But Florida coach Becky Burleigh, with the help of some talented transfers, molded her 4-year-old squad into one of the nation's finest.

Florida struck early on their second shot in the contest. SMU transfer Danielle Fotopolous broke clear down the right side and was tackled just outside the penalty box. The NCAA's all-time leading scorer booted the 18-foot free kick over the wall of defenders and into the net just beyond the fingertips of UNC goalie Siri Mullinix.

The Tar Heel defense tightened, and the Gators managed only 2 more shots in the first half. Meanwhile UNC stepped up the attack and fired 9 shots on Florida's defense. Anna Remy almost tied the game at the 2:46 mark, but Meredith Flaherty, a Clemson transfer, punched the ball away. The Gators led at halftime, 1–0.

Coach Anson Dorrance's team continued to attack Florida aggressively in the second half, taking 12 shots on goal. But the Gators toughened. They allowed only 3 in the game's final 10 minutes. Four corner kicks provided UNC excellent scoring chances, but the 14-time champions couldn't connect.

Florida pushed the rules to the limit. Officials whistled the Gators for 31 fouls compared to 4 for UNC. Fortunately, Flaherty stopped every shot that came her way, and Florida triumphed 1–0. North Carolina failed to capture the NCAA championship for only the third time since the tournament's inception in 1982.

What a surprise. The new kids won. Who would have thought that a tiny, emerging soccer program could produce an NCAA champ? But with an outstanding coach, transplants from good schools, the right conditions, and faith, the Gators did it. The program grew from a tiny seed to a huge tree.

Jesus likened His kingdom to a mustard seed, the smallest God created. But when planted in the right soil and nurtured, the tiny nucleus sprouts and grows into a tree large enough to provide shade and attract birds.

God's kingdom began with just a few. But it's grown big enough to encompass the whole world. With our diligence, God's kingdom can do great and mighty things.

Look in your kitchen's spices. Examine some of the seeds you find: sesame, poppy, coriander, dill, and nutmeg. Maybe you even have mustard seed. Consider the possibilities of each. Praise God for His kingdom and for your potential in it.

ANOTHER MIRACLE ON ICE

Now while he was in Jerusalem at the Passover Feast, many people saw the miraculous signs he was doing and believed in his name. —JOHN 2:23

The United States and Canada squared off in the first women's Olympic hockey championship at the 1998 Nagano (Japan) games. Everyone expected the matchup, and each team knew the other well.

The Canadians and the Americans engaged in a 14-game pre-Olympic exhibition series and evenly split the victories. But the United States gained a slight edge with each competition and posted a 5–2 record over the final 7 games.

In the gold-medal match, both squads played remarkably well in the opening period. The contest featured few penalties and almost nonstop action. The goalies, Canada's Manon Rheaume and U.S.A.'s Sarah Tueting, sparkled.

Dartmouth's Gretchen Ulion scored the game's first goal on a second-period power play. Harvard's Sandra Whyte set up the goal with a terrific peripheral shot.

Canada's Danielle Goyette received a penalty following a collision with Shirley Looney in the third period, and the Americans took immediate advantage of the short skate. Whyte passed from the middle through two defenders to Looney positioned outside the left post. The Northeastern University player shoved the puck into the net before Rheaume could slide over and cover.

A Goyette goal narrowed the U.S. lead to 2–1 with 4 minutes to play. In the final moments, the Canadians pulled Rheaume from the net to attack at full force. But the Americans steered the puck toward the opposition goal. Whyte blasted it into an empty net with 8 seconds remaining for a 3–1 United States victory.

The game's conclusion resembled the American men's 1980 Olympic hockey victory over the Russians. Flags waved, players hugged, and bouquets of flowers rained onto the ice. Many of the 1998 gold medalists admitted they aspired to be hockey players after watching the made-for-television movie about the 1980 men's team, *Miracle on Ice*.

In 1980 at Lake Placid, New York, no one gave the American collegians much of a chance against the stronger, more experienced Russian men. Yet with each contest, the young USA players gained poise, confidence, and game-sense. Shouts of U-S-A, U-S-A, U-S-A rang through the arena. Fans felt chills when the American Davids slew the mighty Russian Goliaths. It was a miracle.

And that miracle inspired a new generation of boys and girls to take up hockey through the movie and stories related by their parents and coaches. Some not yet born and some only small children in 1980 knew they could be part of a miracle gold medal too.

Jesus performed miracles during his earthly life. Many believed in the Savior because of what they saw and experienced.

No one alive today saw Jesus' miracles, yet we trust Him. Some have faith because of Bible stories. Others believe through the witness of their parents or Christian mentors who trusted through the witness of their parents who heard the stories from their parents and so on and so on. We know the miracles of the Bible are true, and we know the miracle of the Holy Spirit in our lives. This is why we believe.

List some of the sports miracle victories you have witnessed or heard about. Did they influence spectator support? List some of Christ's miracles. Thank God for those who followed Him because of His miracles. Praise the Father for those who choose to serve Him today without witnessing those signs.

SCHMIDT SPEARS HER WAY TO RECORD

But an evil spirit from the Lord came upon Saul as he was sitting in his house with his spear in his hand. While David was playing the harp, Saul tried to pin him to the wall with his spear, but David eluded him as Saul drove the spear into the wall. That night David made good his escape.

—1 SAMUEL 19:9-10

Kathy "Kate" Schmidt's youth softball coach encouraged her to try out for the javelin. Her strong throws from center field nailed numerous opponents at the plate before base coaches automatically began holding runners at third.

Kate's inquiries about training for the event brought a lukewarm reception from her parents. Their indifference resolved the Long Beach, California native to become the very best.

Fortunately for the 6-foot, 1-inch athlete, the Long Beach Comets, a local track club, boasted top-notch coaches. Dave Pearson taught her the basics of tossing the spear, and in 1969, the 15 year old won her first of seven American championships.

The following year, Schmidt severely tore a tendon in her elbow with an off-balance throw. The spearchucker endured months of rest followed by many more months of painful rehabilitation.

In the 1972 Munich (Germany) games, Kate heaved the javelin 196 feet, 8 inches (196-8) and earned the bronze, the first javelin medal won by an American woman since Babe Didriksen captured the gold forty years earlier. Although Germany's Ruth Fuchs set an Olympic record with her 209-7 winning throw, the taste of success and the thrill of competing with 10,000 of the worlds' best athletes fueled the 18 year old's desire to improve.

Four years later in Montreal, despite suffering from a nerve tumor in her left arm, Kate increased her distance over 13 feet to 209-10. But Fuchs went to 216-4 for her second straight gold. Schmidt settled for a repeat bronze as Marion Becker hurled 212-3 for the silver.

On September 11, 1977, the Californian participated in a European meet at Furth, Germany. The airlines had lost her javelin, so Kate borrowed. Her final throw sailed and sailed and sailed, coming to rest at 227-5 and eclipsing Fuchs' world record by 8 inches. The American press dubbed Schmidt, "Kate the Great."

Kate Schmidt loved throwing her spear. She traveled the world making three Olympic teams, including the 1980 team that didn't compete, and barely missing in 1984. She won seven national javelin titles. In 1994, the National Track and Field association inducted Kate the Great into its Hall of Fame. She said she found in her sport the joy of "a bucket of iced tea, a sunny afternoon at UCLA, and a bunch of spears."

But others throw the spear in anger with evil intent. Early soldiers carried them as weapons. In the Bible, when King Saul became jealous of David, he attacked him with his spear. He tried to pin the young musician against the wall and attempted to kill him. Fortunately, the future king managed to escape.

Many things in life can be used in joy with intent for good or in anger for evil purposes. God wants us to choose joy.

Consider some objects that can be used for either good or evil. Include materials you own as well as sports equipment such as the javelin, baseball bat, or hockey stick. Thank God for all the items you possess. Ask Him to help you employ them for His positive purposes.

Women's American Basketball League Meets Demise

Jesus said to her, "I am the resurrection and the life. He who believes in me will live, even though he dies; and whosoever lives and believes in me will never die." —JOHN 11:25

In late December 1998, the women's American Basketball League (ABL) ceased operations early in its third year by declaring bankruptcy. Gary Cavalli, the ABL's cofounder, cited lack of television exposure as the primary reason for the demise.

An ABL All-Star Game hosted by the San Jose Lasers had been scheduled for January 24, 1999. A die-hard Laser and ABL fan, Gay Katilius, decided to take matters into her own hands and organized a farewell party for the League called HoopSalute.

Using the power of the Internet and assistance from former Olympian and Laser star Jennifer Azzi, Katilius and her volunteers recruited fifteen ex-ABL players for the game. Former coaches Angela Beck of the Lasers and Lin Dunn of the Portland Power directed the teams dubbed Beck's Bombers and Dunn's Dunkers.

Nearly 2,000 fans crammed into the DeAnza College gym in Cupertino, California, to pay homage to their idols. Ex-Seattle Reign forward Naomi Mulitauapele sang the National Anthem. Halftime entertainment included a slam-dunk exhibition by four-time Olympian Teresa Edwards and a 3-point shooting contest won by Katy Steding. A last-second shot brought victory to the Bombers, 101-100.

At the game's conclusion, Azzi presented Katilius with her Olympic jersey. Former Laser Sheri Sam delivered a tribute to Azzi, Edwards, and Steding, the three 1996 Olympians in attendance. Edwards described her final night representing the ABL as, "a bittersweet end."

The nine-team league began with great promise. During the

inaugural season attendance averaged 3,536, and the Columbus Quest won the championship by defeating the Richmond Rage. The second year saw increased attendance to 4,333 with the Quest repeating with victory over the Long Beach StingRays.

Why did the ABL die? Without television money, teams couldn't make it even with excellent fan support. Although games were televised at various times by SportsChannel Regional Networks, BET, and Fox Sports Net, the women couldn't draw good ratings.

Scheduling games during the traditional college and NBA seasons led to too much competition for viewers. The better-funded WNBA lured players away from the ABL and provided fans basketball during the summer. After two and a half years, the ABL seemed destined to perish though some of the players found resurrection on WNBA teams.

Death is part of life. All people are destined to die. After His close friend passed away, Jesus explained to Lazarus' sister Martha the facts of life, death, and resurrection. Lazarus' sister Mary expressed her faith by weeping that if Jesus had been there, her brother would still be alive. Jesus showed He had power over death by raising Lazarus from the dead four days after his burial.

Through faith in Jesus Christ, death becomes life—life eternal. After we, as Christians, die physically, we live spiritually forever with God. Hallelujah!

Read the account of Lazarus' death in John 11:17-44. Contrast the comments of Mary and the words of Martha. How did Jesus guide each? If you have not yet expressed your faith in Christ, consider doing so. If needed, ask a Christian friend for guidance. Praise God for victory over death in words or song. Thank Him for eternal life.

I wait for you, O Lord; you will answer, O Lord my God. For I said, "Do not let them gloat or exalt themselves over me when my foot slips." For I am about to fall, and my pain is ever with me. —PSALM 38:15-17

No American gymnast ever faced greater expectations than Kim Zmeskal did in the 1992 Barcelona (Spain) Olympics. The 16 year old appeared on the pre-Olympic cover of *Time* magazine, and dozens of articles hailed her as, "America's best hope for gold."

The 1991 All-Round World champion fared badly on opening night. In her first event, the beam, she rushed a tumbling pass and teetered on the edge of the narrow plank. A few seconds later, Kim slipped to the floor and remounted. With a mediocre score of 9.35, coach Bela Karolyi rated her chances of advancing to the all-round competition as remote.

Despite solid scores of 9.925 on the floor exercise, 9.9 in the vault, and 9.887 on the uneven bars, Zmeskal ranked 32nd after the compulsories and fifth on the American squad. Americans Dominique Dawes and Kerri Strug stood between her and the opportunity for an individual medal.

With millions watching worldwide, Kim refused to quit. In the team optionals, the Houston native scored 9.912 on beam, 9.95 on vault, and 9.925 on the floor. She rocketed to twelfth place overall and third among the U.S. gymnasts.

In the long run, Zmeskal's stellar performance insured the United States a team medal. With a combined score of 394.704, the Red, White, and Blue squad captured the bronze, only the second team medal won by the Americans in a non-boycotted Olympics.

Disappointment continued in the overall individual competition, however. During the floor exercise, a weak tumbling pass forced Zmeskal to use a double back dismount instead of a full twisting double back. The added force pushed Kim slightly out-of-bounds.

Although she scored a 9.775, her chances for a medal vanished against the topflight field. Kim finished tenth overall, placing sixth in floor exercise and eighth in vault.

At the Olympics conclusion, Karolyi admitted his pupil had suffered an ankle stress fracture just prior to the games. Yet, the gold-medal hopeful competed through pain. Each movement in every event risked a slip or fall and more serious injury.

As others secretly gloated and silently exalted themselves when they outscored Kim, she maintained her poise. Unlike many athletes, Zmeskal never used the injury as an excuse or cried on the arena floor while watching her marks appear.

Falling when no one is around is one thing. Doing it in front of the whole world is quite another. People often handle disappointment and pain far better privately than they do publicly. Through the media, exposing emotional hurts and failings has become commonplace in today's society.

King David knew the dangers of being a public figure. He committed adultery. Worse, he covered it up by having Bathsheba's husband, Uriah, placed on the battlefield to be killed. He knew the depth of his sin and pain. It was with him every day. But he prayed privately to God for help in his despair.

Read David's prayer in Psalm 38. Scan a daily newspaper or watch a television newscast. Note examples of individuals gloating over the misfortunes of others. Observe situations in which the media seemed to invade personal privacy. Praise God for the love and respect He exhibits for each individual. Ask Him to help you show the same.

WORLD SEES HAMILL WIN GOLD MEDAL

*Then the eyes of those who see will no longer be
closed, and the ears of those who hear will listen.*

—ISAIAH 32:3

Dorothy Hamill received little notoriety compared to previous American figure skating champions. Unlike Carol Heiss or Peggy Fleming, the nearsighted young woman from Riverside, Connecticut, never won a World Championship prior to her Olympic competition.

In the 1976 Innsbruck (Austria) games, experts favored the two previous international winners, East Germany's Christine Errath or the Netherland's Dianne de Leeuw. Although Dorothy captured back-to-back U.S. national crowns in 1974 and 1975, the American rated as a quite unlikely gold medalist.

But the student of Carlo Fassi brought a new style of athleticism to women's figure skating. Unlike the gliding and floating popularized by Fleming and her contemporaries, Dorothy jumped, spun, and flew.

The 19 year old took the early lead in the compulsory figures and moved further ahead in the two-minute short program. Half the scoring remained in the four-minute free skate portion, and a strong showing could bring the gold medal back to the U.S.A.

Dorothy, whose limited financial budget permitted no frills, wore a $75 pink knit dress sewn by a family friend. She skated to melodies from the old Errol Flynn movie *Seahawk* that her father Chalmers, an executive with Pitney Bowes, had taped.

The teenager made one concession to the power of television. For the free skate, she ditched the thick, heavy glasses worn during the compulsory figures in favor of contact lenses. Although they felt uncomfortable and limited her vision, the American with the girl-next-door looks knew appearances meant almost everything in figure skating judging.

Dorothy flawlessly executed her program. Her delayed axel jump, high speed spins, and closing signature move, a spin into a sitspin called the "Hamill camel," brought prolonged cheers and applause.

After her performance, the myopic skater squinted to read her scores. She received 5.8s in technical merit and 5.9s in artistic performance.

The outstanding marks increased Dorothy's lead. When the competition ended six skaters later, America not only welcomed a new Olympic gold medalist, it embraced a new sweetheart as well.

The contact lenses made all the difference just as the thick glasses had before them. The glasses enabled Dorothy Hamill to see the compulsory figures. The contact lenses allowed the judges to see her.

In life, appearances are important even though they may not always be what they seem. Exchanging the glasses for contacts opened the eyes of the judges and the world to Dorothy's talent and beauty. Could she see better? No. Could they see her better? Absolutely!

Many times we close our eyes to the world just as the judges had closed their eyes to Dorothey Hamill. We see our needs, our wants, our friends, our family, our home, and our church. We gravitate toward the familiar and attractive.

But God wants more. He desires that we move from near-sighted, myopic vision to far-sighted, world mission vision. If we ask, the Father will open our eyes to become His eyes.

Examine your attitude toward people who wear glasses. Do you view them as intelligent even though they may be only average? Do you count them as somehow less athletic because of the lenses? Ask God to open your eyes to the needs of the world and to help you respond to reality rather than appearances.

PITOU TURNS AIRPORT CORNER TO MEDAL

Train a child in the way he should go, and when he is old he will not turn from it. —PROVERBS 22:6

At age 5, Penelope "Penny" Pitou skied down her native New Hampshire slopes on barrel staves held in place by large rubber bands. By the time Penny reached high school, she sought only one goal, making the 1956 Olympic ski team.

The driven young woman moved her dream into positive action. She trained for the rigorous events in three-day cycles, biking 25 miles one day, then running 2 miles the next, followed by climbing a mountain on the third.

Penny repeated the workouts over and over and earned a berth on the '56 team. Although she failed to medal, the experience fueled her ambition to improve.

Teammate Betsy Snite and Pitou skipped college and traveled to Europe to work and train. Since the transplanted American spoke German and French, she found a job as a translator in Anton Kastle's Austrian ski factory. In her spare time, she took lessons and practiced.

Penny made the 1960 United States team and trained under David Lawrence in Aspen, Colorado. He kept the ski squad on a strict regime of gymnastics, roadwork, weight training, and low-calorie diets.

In the Squaw Valley, California, games, the women's downhill took place on a mountain designated as KT-22. The slope dropped 1,814 feet vertically followed by a mile run. About three-fourths into the course, contestants faced a nasty 90-degree turn dubbed, "Airplane Corner."

As Penny waited her turn to race, she learned fourteen skiers had crashed while attempting the tricky maneuver. The American finally received her green light and bolted away in a blast of snowy powder.

Pitou survived her downhill and clocked a 1:38.6. She claimed she hadn't tumbled because of the power she felt from competing in the Olympic games. Penny settled for the silver as Germany's Heidi Biebl stayed steady and recorded a 1:37.6.

Americans swept silver in every women's race as Pitou captured another second in the giant slalom, and fellow European traveler Betsy Snite won the regular slalom. The United States women's ski team totaled more medals than any competing country.

That must have been some turn. Ninety degrees is a fourth of a circle. But Penny had been trained since she was a child. Countless hours of practice and conditioning gave her the strength and power to successfully navigate Airplane Corner. While other skiers fell, Pitou held the course.

In athletics, taking up a sport in childhood often yields great rewards. Early training increases the possibility of success and leads to lifelong skills and habits.

The same holds true in the Christian life. Children who understand that God loves them and wants them to love others forever remain secure in His love. Girls and boys who are trained in right living continue the practice. Little ones who learn to pray and depend on God become adults who rely on their Heavenly Father.

If you're in good shape, consider trying Penny's regime for a few days. If not, imagine biking 25 miles, running 2, and then climbing a mountain. Think about what the habit would do for your body. Ask God to help you train little ones in the way they should go. Thank Him for good habits you learned as a child.

Let your eyes gaze straight ahead, fix your gaze directly before you. —PROVERBS 4:25

As a young girl, Carol Blazejowski always carried a basketball to the Cranford, New Jersey, playground. She knew females seldom received a warm reception on the court, but possessing the game ball increased her odds of getting playing time.

Before long, Carol could afford to show up empty-handed. With smooth moves and a keen eye for the basket, the sharpshooter went from wall flower to first-chosen in the pickup league.

Cranford High School didn't field a women's basketball team in 1974. Carol pressured the combination athletic director and basketball coach to add a female squad by trying out for and winning a spot on the men's team.

Because of limited finances, Blazejowski enrolled at Montclair State in nearby Upper Montclair, New Jersey, joining a fledgling non-scholarship basketball program. But over the next four years, "Blaze" and her fellow Red Hawks put the school on the athletic map.

On March 6, 1977, New York's Madison Square Garden scheduled the first big-time women's collegiate basketball doubleheader. Montclair State faced Queens College in the opener, and Delta State drew Immaculata in the second contest. More than 12,000 spectators turned out for the extravaganza.

The Knights of Queens led the Red Hawks by as many as 11 late in the first half. Foul trouble and a sagging defense contained Carol, the nation's leading scorer, to just 14 points.

But after drawing her fourth foul early in the second half, Montclair's coach told the junior forward to forget her usual driving the lane and to shoot nothing but jumpers. Blaze's eagle eye found the mark 17 times in 21 attempts as the Red Hawks defeated the Knights, 102–91. Blazejowski's 52 points set a collegiate Madison Square Garden record unsurpassed to this day.

The three-time All-American scored a career 3,199 points and led the nation in scoring in 1977 with 34.0 points per game and 1978 at 38.6 points per game. Her senior year, Carol led Montclair State to the Final Four of the AIAW Tournament.

Carol Blazejowski became one of the all-time greatest scorers in women's basketball. What was her secret? It began with practice. She spent hours and hours shooting in the driveway and on the playground.

She chose to challenge herself by opposing tougher, stronger, and more experienced competition. She played pick-up games with the boys whenever she could. When she couldn't, she spent the time imagining defenders.

Blaze also learned to keep her eyes gazing straight ahead at the basket. She made scoring her goal and kept her body and her heart always moving toward her aim.

God wants us to set the goal of following His ways completely throughout our lives. But once set, do we wander around the target without getting close? Or do we focus our eyes looking straight ahead directed toward our aim? Do we keep our bodies and hearts in line with the Father's practice? Or do we sometimes compete on Satan's team?

Only when we fix our eyes on Jesus Christ can we become like Him.

Practice shooting a basketball. First, throw the ball up a few times without watching the basket. Did you make many shots? Then, keep your eyes fixed on the hoop. Better? Ask God to help you keep your gaze on Him.

SPEEDSTER TYUS OVERSHADOWS COMPETITORS

*Because you are my help, I sing in the shadow of
your wings. I stay close to you; your right hand
upholds me.* —PSALM 63:7-8

Wyomia Tyus' three older brothers overshadowed her
throughout childhood. The Griffin, Georgia, native never
realized her athletic potential until she reached high school.

Tennessee State track coach Ed Temple noticed Wyomia at a
1961 Georgia meet and invited the 15 year old to his summer
camp. Two years later he offered Tyus a collegiate scholarship.

The sprinter developed quickly but always finished behind fellow Tigerbelle Edith McGuire. Surprisingly at age 19, Wyomia
qualified for the 1964 Tokyo (Japan) Olympics.

The press focused on McGuire, and Wyomia willingly stayed on
the sidelines. But in the 100 meters the incredible occurred. In
the second round, Tyus dropped her personal best from 11.5 seconds to 11.2, tying Wilma Rudolph's world record. With that victory behind her, she easily defeated McGuire in the finals for only
the second time ever and claimed the gold by a 2-meter margin.

Though urged by her family to retire from running, the
Tennessee State star continued to race for pure enjoyment. She
qualified for the Olympics a second time and competed in the
1968 Mexico City Games.

Friends cautioned Wyomia about the "repeat jinx." No 100-
meter sprinter, male or female, had ever captured back-to-back
gold medals.

Keen competition for the 100-meter crown prevailed in
Mexico's mile-high atmosphere. In the first round, three
Americans—Tyus, Margaret Bailes, and Barbara Ferrell—tied the
Olympic mark of 11.2. The second round witnessed Ferrell and
Irena Szewinska equal the world record of 11.1, but Wyomia
went .1 better with a wind-aided 11.0.

Oddsmakers couldn't settle on a favorite in the finals. Four runners—Tyus, Ferrell, Bailes, and Szewinska—who held personal bests of 11.1, competed in the field of eight.

But at the finish line, Wyomia clearly led the pack. Using electronic timing devices that measured hundredths of seconds, she established a new world's record of 11.08 and became the first 100-meter sprinter to capture consecutive golds. America's Gail Devers later matched her feat with double victories in 1992 and 1996.

Tyus seemed to be always in other people's shadows. She spent her childhood and early teens in the shadows of three older brothers. Then most people overlooked her at Tennessee State with Edith McGuire always out in front.

Finally, Wyomia Tyus emerged to stand atop the Olympic medal stand singing "The Star Spangled Banner." The shadows were gone, but they had enabled her to train out of the spotlight but with the goal clearly ahead and in sight.

The psalmist David compared God's care to staying in the shadow of His wings. The Father keeps us safe while enabling us to touch the potential He has given us. He remains ahead but near enough to help us reach our goals.

Think of the people who have overshadowed you. Perhaps you felt brothers, sisters, or cousins got all the attention. Maybe an athletic, academic, or music competitor gained the glory while you did just okay. Then consider how you reacted. Did you work harder to get out of the shadow? Did you find the pressure off you because it was on them? Thank God for keeping you in His shadow. Ask Him to help you find the positive in situations when you're overshadowed.

AMERICAN SOCCER BLOSSOMS IN TITLE GAME

I will be like the dew to Israel; he will blossom like a lily. Like a cedar of Lebanon he will send down his roots; his young shoots will grow. —HOSEA 14:5

It seems Kristine Lilly breaks a world record every time she steps onto the soccer field. The former University of North Carolina star has made thousands of plays in 186 tournament matches. But a single moment in the 1999 Women's World Cup shines above all others.

The United States hosted China in the title game. A standing-room-only audience of 90,815 packed Pasadena's Rose Bowl. Capacity crowds on both coasts and in America's heartland had attended the elimination matches, and the final contest took on an aura of a Super Bowl or World Series.

For 90 minutes both teams battled, keeping their defenders back to prevent goals off counterattacks. Regulation play ended in a 0–0 tie, and the match went to a 15-minute sudden-death period. A goal scored by either team meant victory.

After the 90th minute, Michelle Akers succumbed to exhaustion. With the best American defender on the bench, the Chinese increased their aggressiveness, and the United States fell back on their heels.

In the first overtime period, China's Liu Ying sent a corner kick from the left side to the front of the U.S. goal. Fan Yunjie headed the ball perfectly, and for a brief moment it appeared American's newfound heroines would suffer an agonizing defeat.

But suddenly, Kristine Lilly headed the ball away from the goal and into the open field. Positioned inside the near post, her incredible play kept the host team's hopes alive.

The first overtime ended at 0–0, and another 15-minute period began. A pep talk by Carla Overbeck and Julie Foudy during the break fueled the American resolve, and the second overtime again concluded with the score tied at zero.

After two scoreless overtimes, penalty kicks would decide the outcome. Teams would alternate kicks by five different players. With the shots even at 2–2, goalie Briana Scurry guessed Lui Ying would pull her kick to the right. The American goalkeeper's premonition was correct. Scurry hit the ball with both hands, and it bounced harmlessly away.

The United States made good on its final three shots with Brandi Chastain nailing number five. By a 5–4 penalty kick margin, the U.S.A. captured its second Women's World Cup.

The exuberant team mobbed Brandi. The largest crowd ever to see a women's sporting event roared. Fans watching by television celebrated. Young, soccer-playing girls across the country chose their favorite American team members to idolize as they began practice and games with new inspiration.

Women's soccer blossomed that day and began to put down roots for further growth.

God's love provides that same kind of overwhelming growth and inspiration in our lives. He promises to be like the morning dew that gives moisture, coolness, and nourishment to beautiful flowers and fragrant trees. The Creator roots us firmly in His truth and blesses us with His Word. He dwells with us in worship and guides us through prayer.

Spend some time on a soccer field. Try a soccer header, hitting the ball with your head, to make it change course. Attempt to kick a goal, trying not to let the goalie know your chosen direction. Thank God for providing nourishing growth and direction in your life.

TOP *Bridget DiCave plays collegiate basketball at age 38.* (SEE PAGE 180)

BOTTOM *Charlotte Smith sinks an incredible three-pointer to win the 1994 NCAA basketball final.* (SEE PAGE 188)

Hall of Famer Juli Inkster wins 1999 United States Open with record score.
(SEE PAGE 108)

COURTESY JULIE HARRINGTON

COURTESY UNIVERSITY OF ARKANSAS

TOP *Julie Harrington trades the tennis court for the courtroom.* (SEE PAGE 198)

BOTTOM *Christy Smith learns to play basketball among the cornfields.*
(SEE PAGE 196)

COURTESY UNIVERSITY OF NORTH CAROLINA

COURTESY PAT McCORMICK EDUCATIONAL FOUNDATION

TOP *Marion Jones excels at basketball and track.* (SEE PAGE 202)

BOTTOM *Pat McCormick dives for Olympic gold.* (SEE PAGE 208)

Mia Hamm shines at every level of soccer competition. (SEE PAGE 176)

COURTESY DAN WIZA / MADISON BLACK WOLF

COURTESY BALL STATE UNIVERSITY

TOP *Ila Borders believes a diamond is a girl's best friend.* (SEE PAGE 214)

BOTTOM *LaTasha Jenkins loves running and writing.* (SEE PAGE 216)

> *Oh, for the days when I was in my prime, when God's intimate friendship blessed my house.* — JOB 29:4

Maureen Connolly loved horses, but her divorced mother couldn't afford riding lessons. The San Diego, California native turned to tennis instead.

Trained by Eleanor Tennant, Maureen traveled cross country to capture the junior United States championship in 1949 and 1950. She also entered the United States Open both years, falling in the second round.

But in 1951, the master of baseline ground strokes reached her prime at Forest Hills. Down 1–4 in the first set of the semifinals, she rallied to defeat the top seed, Doris Hart, 6–4, 6–4. In the finals against second seed Shirley Fry, Maureen triumphed 6–3, 1–6, 6–4. The press dubbed her, "Little Mo," comparing the velocity of her stroke to the big guns of the World War II *Battleship Missouri*, also known as "Big Mo."

From 1951 to 1954, Connolly won nine Grand Slam events, including three United States Opens, three Wimbledons, two French Opens, and one Australian Open. In 1953, Maureen won all four major tournaments, becoming the first woman to achieve the feat. Other than her 2 early losses in the U.S. Open, "Little Mo" tallied a perfect record of 51 match victories in Grand Slam competition.

But two weeks following her 1954 Wimbledon victory, tragedy ended Maureen's stellar career. While horseback riding, a cement truck brushed against her. Thrown to the ground, the tennis star injured her leg so severely she could no longer engage top-ranked competition.

Married to Norman Brinker, a member of the 1952 United States Olympic equestrian team, the couple settled in Dallas, Texas. "Little Mo" dedicated her talents to teaching young players, and in 1968 established the Maureen Connolly Brinker Foundation to promote junior tennis.

Six months later, Maureen died of cancer at age 34. The Maureen Connolly Brinker Cup, a continuing international competition between the United States and Great Britain for young women under age 21, honors her memory.

Surely Maureen longed for the days of Grand Slam tennis competition. She probably lived with what-ifs and what-might-have-beens. Could she have been the greatest women's tennis player of all time? Could she have set records not to be broken for years and years? But she made the most of her days by helping girls perfect their games.

Then when facing cancer treatment and death, she simply longed for normal friendship-filled days in her home. Yet Little Mo left a legacy of grace and dedication to her sport.

It seemed so unjust—a great tennis player taken prematurely away from the game she loved. And then the ultimate unfairness—cancer diagnosis and death at a too-early age.

When tragedies occur and death strikes too soon, we find ourselves asking why. But God never promised His children answers. He never said life would be fair. The Father never assured us of long lives or freedom from pain. He simply promised His presence in bearing all life brings and taking us to live in His house forever when life ends.

Is there a family in your church or community who has experienced tragedy or is facing the premature death of one of its members through cancer or other illness? Watch for ways that you can offer loving support. Ask God to make His presence felt clearly to those experiencing tragedy and loss.

When I smiled at them, they scarcely believed it; the light of my face was precious to them. —JOB 29:24

Golf fans will never forget the wonder and magic that accompanied Nancy Lopez's 1978 rookie year on the Ladies Professional Golf Association (LPGA) tour. After two years at the University of Tulsa, the young woman turned professional and immediately impacted the LPGA. She finished second in four of her first six tournaments, but those runner-up slots simply foreshadowed her potential greatness.

In late February, the 21 year old garnered her first tour victory and followed it with another in early March. Two months later, the woman with the dark, flashing eyes and ever-present smile zoomed into the public spotlight with unparalleled brilliance.

On May 12, the daughter of a Roswell, New Mexico, auto shop operator won the Greater Baltimore Classic by 3 strokes over Donna Caponi. Lopez brought home the first-place trophy the next week in the Coca-Cola Classic, defeating JoAnne Carner in a playoff. Nancy's incredible third title a week later in the Golden Lights Championship brought the LPGA tour off the sports section's back pages and into the headlines.

The dark-haired pro not only captured the media's attention, but she also won the public's heart. Mobs surrounded her on every hole, and she thrived on the pressure. No one ever heard a cross word or saw a frown. Nancy honored every autograph request and made each fan feel important.

Lopez wisely skipped the Peter Jackson Classic to rest for the LPGA Championship. With hundreds packing the gallery and millions watching on television, the Hispanic golfer shot a 13-under-par 275 for her fourth title in a row. Unfazed by the media circus, Nancy extended her string to 5 at the Bankers Trust Classic.

The streak ended a week later at the Lady Keystone Open as the LPGA rookie's concentration waned. She quickly recovered and snared 2 more wins to finish the year with 9, the most since Kathy Whitworth took 10 in 1968.

Her rookie year wasn't a fluke. Lopez won eight events in 1979 during her second season, giving her 17 career victories before age 23. Through the next 20 years, the LPGA Hall of Famer totaled 48 wins, moving to sixth on the all-time list.

Nancy Lopez lit up ladies' professional golf with her presence. She won their hearts with her smile. They loved how she made each feel precious when signing autographs or doing interviews. She achieved greatness, not only on the golf course but also in the galleries.

Some people make us feel good simply because of their presence. They offer sincere smiles, wise words, and loving laughter. When we're with them, life seems easier and less stress-filled.

God made each of us His precious creation. He smiles on our days and lights our faces with His presence. In turn, the Father wants us to do the same. He desires that we treat all His children with love and smiles. The Lord asks that we let His light shine through us to others. He wants us to wake each morning with the prayer that we will make every person we see glad they were with us.

Determine that you will focus your full attention on the persons you meet during the day. Don't forget the sales clerk, the mail carrier, and others whose names you don't know. Smile. Be positive, but remember they may be grieving or experiencing tough times or tragedy. Try to let God's light shine through you. Praise God for all His children everywhere.

I was personally unknown to the churches of Judea that are in Christ. They only heard the report: "The man who formerly persecuted us is now preaching the faith he once tried to destroy." —GALATIANS 1:22-23

Few people ever saw America's greatest woman basketball player of the 1950s and 1960s. Nera White, who played for Nashville Business College (NBC) from 1955 to 1969, performed in an era when newspaper coverage meant a scant paragraph or two, and television exposure didn't exist for women's collegiate teams.

Wealthy Nashville businessman, Herman O. Balls, operated a printing shop and sponsored the NBC team as a hobby. He attracted the young woman who grew up on a farm 100 miles northeast of Nashville with an offer of room and board while she attended Peabody College for Teachers.

Since the Amateur Athletic Union (AAU), the governing body for women's sports at that time, permitted unlimited eligibility, Ball employed White after graduation, and she continued as the team's star. NBC won ten AAU national titles, including eight straight from 1962 to 1969. The former Tennessee farm girl won the National Tournament's Most Valuable Player Award ten times.

Under the archaic AAU women's rules with six players to a side, two remained fixed in the offensive zone, two in the defensive zone, and two roamed the court. The 6-foot, 1-inch combination guard/center played the game to perfection.

Positioned under the basket on defense, White could snag a rebound, key the fast break, and catch up with a ball on the opposite end. At point guard, she shot long-range jumpers and drove the lane with equal skill. If an opponent collapsed around her, the female superstar passed to an open teammate for an easy basket.

Sue Gunter, former teammate and later coach at Louisiana State University, recalled Nera could drive both ways, reverse dribble, hit a 30-foot hook shot, and dunk. Yet, the floor leader received more satisfaction in making an assist than in hitting a shot.

But times changed. American women's basketball adopted five-on-five rules similar to men's and women's international competition. Balls disbanded his team rather than flow with the changes, and White retired from the game.

NBC's sponsor died in 1982, and two nephews took over the printing business. Citing lack of work, they discharged White with two months severance pay. The 10-time AAU MVP returned to the family farm she inherited outside Lafayette, Tennessee. In 1992, the National Basketball Hall of Fame named Nera White and Delta State's Lusia Harris as its first two women inductees.

Many Americans today, including serious basketball fans, have never heard of White. Even those who followed the sport in the 1950s and 1960s never saw her play. People didn't personally know the great star. But they heard the reports. They knew her reputation. Nera White made the Hall of Fame.

The Apostle Paul wasn't personally known among Christians. But they had heard the reports. They knew his reputation. He preached the faith as fervently as he had persecuted it.

People who don't personally know us often have heard of us. Our reputation precedes us and follows us. The Heavenly Father wants it to be a valuable one.

Name famous college or professional athletes you know. Did you choose those you've met personally or simply those you've watched play and know by reputation? Does reputation color how you feel about them? Ask God to help you maintain a Christian reputation.

But because my servant Caleb has a different spirit and follows me wholeheartedly, I will bring him into the land he went to, and his descendants will inherit it.

—NUMBERS 14:24

Lynn Jennings refused to be confined by convention. She won the 1977 high school cross country championship despite attending a school that didn't field a women's team. As a 17 year old, Jennings unofficially ran in the Boston Marathon, clocking in a 2:46.

As Jennings matured as a runner, she concentrated on the 10,000 meters, the first American woman to devote herself to the event. Lynn qualified for the 10K in three consecutive Olympics: 1988, 1992, and 1996. At the 1992 Barcelona (Spain) games, she captured the bronze medal, running the course in just over 30 minutes and setting an American record of 31:19.89.

In 1999, the three-time world cross country champion switched to the marathon. She selected Boston as her first major competition, returning to the site after 22 years. Jennings set a sub-2:42 time as her goal. That clocking would qualify her for the 1999 Olympic Marathon Trials.

Lynn ran alongside South Africa's Colleen De Reuck for the first 8 1/2 miles. Then she competed alone, discouraged by the lack of female companionship.

At the 15-mile mark, Lynn struggled. Her legs felt heavy, her stomach and rib cage tightened, and her mind fought against quitting. But her coach John Babington and fans encouraged the 39-year-old runner. She resolved to finish.

The Olympian crossed the line exhausted and wobbled into the Copley Plaza Hotel's recovery area where doctors discovered her body temperature had dropped to 96 degrees. The medical staff wrapped Lynn in an air bag and blew warm air over her body. She received an IV to replace lost fluid.

A short time later, Jennings had recovered sufficiently to mount the podium to answer questions from the press. She had completed the 26 miles in a time of 2:38.37, achieving her sub-2:42 objective and a spot in the trials.

Lynn knew what she wanted, and she didn't mind being distinctive to get it. In high school, she ran alone or with the guys when there wasn't a girls' team. She worked toward the 10,000 meters when no other American woman did. Jennings left other females behind in Boston. Her willing difference earned her medal stands.

In the Old Testament, Caleb didn't mind being different either. Moses sent twelve men to explore Canaan. All agreed on the richness of the land, but ten felt the inhabitants too fierce to defeat. Only two, Caleb and Joshua, believed God would lead the Israelites to victory.

Caleb took a different stand and received his reward. The Lord promised the young man he would survive to enter Canaan and his descendants would inherit the rich land.

God doesn't want us to be different for difference's sake. But He does want us to have the courage to stand for Him even if it means being different.

History pages are filled with stories of individuals who took different stands. In 1955, African-American Rosa Lee Parks refused to give up her seat to a white passenger on an Alabama bus. She helped bring about civil rights. In the late 1800s, Jane Addams' work brought limits to child labor and began efforts toward humane treatment of working women. Recall others who dared to be different. Ask God to give you courage to stand alone when necessary.

SOCCER STAR SHINES AS YOUTH AND ADULT

Those who are wise will shine like the brightness of the heavens, and those who lead many to righteousness, like the stars for ever and ever. —DANIEL 12:3

After watching Mia Hamm in a youth tournament, a coach from the University of North Texas sent word to Coach Anson Dorrance at the University of North Carolina. The head of the women's UNC soccer program traveled to Texas and marveled at what he saw.

The 15 year old accelerated so quickly that she left everyone else on the field behind. Hamm controlled the ball with power and precision more akin to a collegian than a teen.

Dorrance recruited the young woman to UNC. Mia Hamm led North Carolina to NCAA championships in 1989, 1990, 1992, and 1993. In 1991, she skipped a year to train with the United States National Team that ultimately won the first Women's World Cup. Mia tallied 103 goals during her collegiate career, making her the number one Atlantic Coast Conference scorer.

After graduation, the all-star forward continued to play international competition. As a tune-up for the 1999 Women's World cup, Nike sponsored a series of matches in the United States. On May 16, the Americans hosted Holland at Chicago's Soldier Field.

In the 53rd minute of the game, Mia took a pass from Cindy Parlow at the top of the penalty box. She dribbled to her left, rode off an attempted tackle, faked a shot, and then stroked a left-footed 16-yard bullet into the net. The goal, number 107 of Hamm's international career, tied Italian legend Elisabetta Vignotto for the scoring record.

Less than a week later, the United States faced Brazil in Orlando. With the score tied 0–0 in the waning seconds of the first half, Michelle Akers lofted a pass to Hamm 40 yards away from the goal.

Mia headed the ball to Kristine Lilly who passed to Cindy Parlow at the top of the penalty box. Parlow dribbled momentarily then nailed a perfect pass to Hamm, cutting toward the goal. The forward evaded her defender and blasted a shot through the legs of the Brazilian goalie for the record-breaking goal number 108.

The American bench emptied onto the field to congratulate soccer's all-time leading scorer. Captain Carla Overbeck retrieved the ball and presented it to her teammate of 11 years.

Mia Hamm shone brightly on the soccer scene during her early youth years. She clearly possessed the quickness and athleticism to earn a college scholarship and become a star. Throughout her college years, the UNC Tar Heel lived up to her potential, leading her team to national championships all four years.

And then Hamm moved higher onto the international scene. Again, she played a key role and eventually helped lead her team to win the World Cup. She shone on television, both in soccer games and in commercials. Mia Hamm had clearly become a bright star in both the American and international sky.

Most of us will never star as collegiate athletes. Fewer still will become prominent in sports on the international level. But God says every Christian can shine brightly. We can illuminate the world with our wisdom. We can sparkle forever as we lead others into righteousness through knowing Christ.

Watch television commercials and newspaper or magazine ads for athletes. Why do you think the companies choose them to sell their products? Why do you think God chose you to tell the world about Him? Thank the Heavenly Father for allowing you to be part of His plan to bring righteousness to the world. Ask Him to help you tell others about His saving grace.

FIRMLY ROOTED SWIMMER PLANTS WELL-ROUNDED LIFE

But blessed is the man who trusts in the Lord, whose confidence is in Him. He will be like a tree planted by the water that sends out its roots by the stream. It does not fear when heat comes; its leaves are always green. It has no worries in a year of drought and never fails to bear fruit. —JEREMIAH 17:7-8.

At age 12, Chris von Saltza narrowly missed a spot on the 1956 United States Olympic swimming team. But rather than focus entirely on the 1960 Rome (Italy) games, the youthful swimmer participated in a variety of teenage activities.

Her father, a San Francisco physician, played football and swam in college. He encouraged multiple endeavors, recognizing that too much emphasis on a single sport would deprive his daughter of a well-rounded education.

At Los Gatos High School, Chris earned straight A's, served as class secretary, and waved pom-poms as a cheerleader. School officials marveled at her ability to manage time and organize events. Except for pool water tinting her blonde hair slightly green, the teen never complained about practicing long hours in the water or the painful physical demands of her schedule.

Von Saltza's intensive but well-structured training earned the 16 year old a slot on the 1960 squad. Chris burst on the Rome scene, almost upsetting world record holder Dawn Fraser in the 100-meter freestyle, but she had to settle for the silver.

Later, the American set an Olympic record of 4:50.6 in the 400-meter freestyle and won her first gold medal. In her final events, world records fell as the California cheerleader and her teammates combined to capture gold in two relays, the 4 x 100 freestyle and 4 x 100 medley.

With one silver and three gold medals, Chris returned to the United States, graduated from high school, and entered Stanford University. In 1963, she took a year's leave from her collegiate stud-

ies to work in Asia for the State Department. The former Olympian set up swimming programs as a prelude to the 1964 Tokyo (Japan) Olympic games.

With competitive swimming behind her, Chris returned to Stanford to earn a bachelor's degree in Asian Studies. She later completed a master's in Chinese Studies at the University of California at Berkeley. Von Saltza eventually accepted a position at IBM as a systems analyst, working for the company 25 years before retirement.

With today's prima donna athletes who focus their energies and interests solely on themselves and their sports, Chris von Saltza's career seems unusual. With her father's blessing, she chose to live the life of a normal teen. She studied hard, participated in fun extracurricular activities, and served her school.

Chris' athletic career, completed by four Olympic medals, added to her life but didn't consume it. She put down deep roots for the future. She prepared for life after swimming but used her sport to help Asians and to study their part of the world.

We often spend our time consumed by a sport, job, volunteer or extracurricular activity, or even another person. We narrowly focus our energies and forget to trust God while we prepare for tomorrow. Then, when difficult days come, we find ourselves blown about by the world without needed reserves to weather personal droughts or storms.

Instead, God desires that we put down deep roots in Him through prayer, Bible study, worship, and fellowship with other Christians.

Examine some tree and plant roots in your yard or in a park. After high winds or a storm, notice uprooted trees. How deep were the roots? Praise God for the confidence He gives. Ask Him to help you take time to become deeply rooted in Him.

MOTHER AND DAUGHTER SHARE COMMON COLLEGIATE COMPETITION

As apostles of Christ we could have been a burden to you, but we were gentle among you, like a mother caring for her little children. We loved you so much that we were delighted to share with you not only the gospel of God but our lives as well, because you had become so dear to us. —1 THESSALONIANS 2:7-8

Bridget DiCave enrolled at Pennsylvania's West Chester University at age 36. Not only did the divorced mother of three seek a college education, she also wanted to play basketball.

DiCave walked onto the Golden Ram squad, but Coach Dierde Kane cut the point guard. Because of her skills and ambition, Kane offered the 36 year old a position as a volunteer coach.

In Bridget's third year, West Chester lost two guards, Sue Molnar and Dawn Carter, to early season injuries. With the roster depleted, Coach Kane needed backups. With DiCave's experience and knowledge of the playbook, she became a logical replacement.

After conferring with university officials, the NCAA ruled Bridget eligible for competition and classified her as a sophomore. On January 9, 1999, the 38 year old entered her first collegiate game against Mansfield University. She totaled 2 minutes of action in the 69–43 victory, making a steal and an assist.

In the following contest, the 5-foot play maker tallied her greatest number of minutes with 8 against Columbia Union. DiCave grabbed a rebound and made 2 assists in the 98–29 rout. The nontraditional student made six more appearances for the Golden Rams during the season. Although she never took a shot, she played 23 minutes, totaling 4 rebounds and 4 assists.

In making the transition from coach to player, Bridget became the second member of the DiCave household to compete at an

NCAA institution during the 1998-99 campaign. Her freshman daughter Megan played basketball at Virginia Wesleyan, making them the first simultaneous mother-daughter combination in NCAA history.

Just imagine what character it took for Bridget DiCave to return to college where most students were just over half her age and young enough to be her children. Then think about her courage trying out for basketball. She didn't quite make the team, but she became a caring coach.

Then DiCave took an unfortunate team situation and made it a fortunate personal one. She shared herself and became a real part of the Golden Rams.

As mother and daughter, Bridget and Megan shared not only family but also the common adventure of college basketball. Each knew what the other experienced. And the sharing made college athletics dearer.

Parents teach children to share. In the beginning girls and boys see sharing as giving up. They give up sole possession of toys. They get only half the candy.

But as the Apostle Paul knew, sharing becomes delightful. It creates close relationships and dear bonds. Eventually the toys offer more fun when played with a friend. Half a slice of cake eaten with a family member tastes better than a whole piece eaten alone.

God wants us to share with others, not only ourselves but also the good news of His salvation.

Walk or shoot hoops with a friend or family member. Afterward, visit as you cool down with a drink of cold water. Thank God for the joy of sharing. Ask Him to help you share His Gospel.

"Woe to the obstinate children," declares the Lord, *"to those who carry out plans that are not mine, forming an alliance, but not by my Spirit, heaping sin upon sin."*

—ISAIAH 30:1

Althea Gibson described her childhood as mischievous but not bad. Skipping school, petty shoplifting, and partying all night became routine as she grew up in pre-World War II Harlem.

But concerned adults changed Althea's life. Jazz musician Buddy Walker introduced the 14 year old to Fred Johnson, coach of the Cosmopolitan Tennis Club. The young girl proved to be a natural match with the game.

The native South Carolinian who left her home state at age three enjoyed her lessons but rebelled at the game's strict rules of etiquette. Despite her strong will, Gibson excelled at tennis. She played in four American Tennis Association (ATA) national tournaments during her teen years.

After her 1946 appearance in the organization of primarily black players, two tennis-playing doctors, Hubert A. Eaton and Robert W. Johnson, changed Althea's life forever. They offered to help the young prospect obtain a college scholarship. Unfortunately, Gibson had to inform them that she had not completed high school.

The kindhearted physicians devised an alternate plan. The New York City girl would live in Wilmington, North Carolina, with Dr. Eaton, attend high school, and practice on the Eaton family's private court. During summers she would travel to Lynchburg, Virginia, and play the ATA circuit under Dr. Johnson's supervision.

With only a few minor glitches, their plan worked to perfection. Gibson graduated, enrolled at Florida A&M, and won the first of her 10 straight ATA singles championships in 1947. In 1949, the United States Lawn Tennis Association (USLTA) opened their tournaments to Althea. A year later she played in her first United States National Tennis Championship, the forerunner of the U.S. Open.

Gibson won back-to-back Wimbledon singles titles and U.S. championships in 1957 and 1958, becoming the first major black player. The tennis star turned pro after her second American title and later appeared primarily as an opening act for the Harlem Globetrotters.

When she entered her teen years, Althea drifted. She made her own plans, plans that led her away from an education and a stable career. She did exactly what she wanted, enjoying the moment rather than preparing for the future.

Fortunately, the Lord put concerned adults in her path. Their caring actions changed Gibson's present and future. She put away her obstinance and strong will for the love of tennis. Buddy Walker, Fred Johnson, Hubert Eaton, and Robert Johnson made all the difference in Althea Gibson's life.

Many young women and men stubbornly make plans and behave in ways that displease God. They are led by selfishness rather than the Holy Spirit. Some sacrifice future prospects for present fun. But that's not what God wants. He wants caring adults to put love into action to gently guide youth. And He desires that the youth allow themselves to be mentored into future hope in Him.

Consider mentoring a younger person who needs love and direction. If you feel you're the one who requires assistance, identify an older Christian to help you plan for your future. Praise God for mature adults who put their love into action to assist others.

TRIATHLON TESTS PERSEVERANCE

Blessed is the man who perseveres under trial, because when he has stood the test, he will receive the crown of life that God has promised to those who love him.

—JAMES 1:12

The "Ironman Triathlon" originated from an argument about which athletes had greater strength: swimmers, bikers, or runners. Career navy man, John Collins, proposed a contest to settle the debate. Competitors would swim 2.4 miles, bike 145 miles, and run 26.2 miles.

Collins scheduled the first triathlon on February 18, 1978, in and around Honolulu. He and eleven others completed the course with Gordon Haller, a taxi cab driver, leading the dozen in 11 hours, 48 minutes, and 58 seconds.

The event's founder organized another competition the following year with fifteen participants. Lyn Lemaine, a Boston cyclist, placed sixth overall but first among the females, becoming the first "ironwoman."

Barry McDermott, a *Sports Illustrated* golf writer, covered the event on a whim. His story publicized triathlon, and the participants grew into the hundreds. Beginning in 1980, ABC television filmed portions for their "Wide World of Sports" program, increasing both the public's awareness and triathlon's appeal.

Triathlon's signature moment occurred in 1982. With the men's winner already determined, ABC zeroed in on the women's leader, Julie Moss. The San Diego lifeguard had never competed in an ironman competition, but her rigorous lifesaving training propelled her to a large lead after the swimming and biking competition.

The 23 year old slowed in the running segment but still led by several minutes with only a quarter mile remaining. Suddenly, the young woman fell and needed several minutes to struggle to her feet. Julie wobbled forward and fell again less than 100 yards from the finish line. She regained her footing and stumbled toward the tape, collapsing once more only 50 feet from victory.

After her third fall, Moss could not rise. She desperately crawled toward the tape, but before she could reach it, another San Diego college student, Kathleen McCartney, passed her to claim the crown.

So close, and yet so far. Julie Moss decided to prove her physical strength. She wanted to win the ironwoman crown. She didn't quite earn the victory, but she completed the race. She persevered under the grueling physical trial. Julie crossed the finish line on scraped and scarred hands and knees, but she finished. She didn't win, but she stood the test.

God never promised an easy life to His followers. Instead, He assured us of trials and temptations. James, a servant of God, wrote of the testing his Christian brothers and sisters would face. He knew that hardships would make us stronger. In the Bible, he penned the words that we should count our trials joy because they would develop our perseverance.

We may end life battered with scraped knees, scratched arms, and bruised hearts. But if we persevere in love with the Heavenly Father, we will receive the crown of life God has promised.

Watch the triathlon on television. Were you impressed by the strength and perseverance of the competitors? Would you ever consider entering such an event? Remember, you face more tests in everyday life than you ever will in an athletic contest. Read James 1:2-4. Ask God to help you persevere when you face trials in life.

Proclaim this among the nations: Prepare for war! Rouse the warriors! Let all the fighting men draw near and attack. —JOEL 3:9

As major and minor league baseball struggled during World War II with most of the players fighting in the armed forces, Chicago Cubs owner Phil Wrigley had an idea. He devised an alternative—professional women's softball. He proposed the concept to his fellow owners, but they rejected his plan.

Wrigley then turned to the Midwestern cities with booming wartime industries near Chicago. In 1943, he formed the All American Girls Softball League with four franchises: Kenosha (Wisconsin) Comets, Racine (Wisconsin) Belles, Rockford (Illinois) Peaches, and South Bend (Indiana) Blue Sox.

The league modified traditional softball rules to tailor the game more like baseball. Runners could lead off their bases, and the basepaths extended to 70 feet rather than 60.

Young women flocked from all over the United States and Canada to compete for the fewer than 100 available slots. Playing a 108-game schedule, the league drew 175,000 fans, and at mid-season, Wrigley changed the name to the All American Girls Professional Baseball League (AAGPBL).

The women's high caliber of play fueled the league's popularity. The AAGPBL added new teams, the Milwaukee (Wisconsin) Chicks and Fort Wayne (Indiana) Daisies, in 1944 and 1945.

Many believed women's baseball would fade when the troops returned from World War II and the major league teams regained their strength. But the Midwestern industrial towns continued to support the AAGPBL.

Two more teams, the Muskogen (Michigan) Lassies and Peoria (Illinois) Red Wings, joined in 1946, and the league reached a ten-team peak in 1948 with the addition of the Chicago (Illinois) Colleens and the Springfield (Illinois) Sallies. Almost 1 million fans attended the women's games that year.

But in the 1950s, interest waned. Competition from television and expansion by major league baseball into the Midwest eroded the league's strength. After very low attendance in 1954, the AAGPBL folded.

Curiosity about women's baseball rose in the 1980s. The National Baseball Hall of Fame opened an exhibit on "Women in Baseball," and Penny Marshall directed an award-winning motion picture based on the AAGPBL titled *A League of Their Own*.

The league developed because men were gone to war, defending liberty around the world. The women were home, and Americans still loved their national pastime.

In the abnormal days of fighting with rationing of gasoline, tires, sugar, and many other goods, the games made life seem more normal. With bad news telegrams regularly arriving containing notices of loved ones wounded or dead, women's baseball provided an escape.

The Bible talks of war. God never makes fighting His first choice of action. But He does condone it to preserve His people's land, religious practices, and freedom. The Lord wants us to seek peace without fearing war.

Check your local library for a copy of A Whole New Ball Game: The Story of the All-American Girls Professional Baseball League by Sue Macy. Talk to someone who was alive during World War II about their memories of rationing and daily life in America. Praise God for freedom. Ask Him to keep the world at peace.

UNC Coach Makes Surprising Choice for Final Shot

For you are a people holy to the Lord your God. The Lord your God has chosen you out of all the peoples on the face of the earth to be his people, his treasured possession.

—DEUTERONOMY 7:6

Trailing Louisiana Tech, 59–57, with 0.7 seconds remaining in the 1994 NCAA basketball finals, North Carolina (UNC) Coach Sylvia Hatchell selected a game-winning play. Her choice surprised everyone, including the shooter.

Almost 12,000 fans packed the Richmond Coliseum for the championship contest. North Carolina led, 48–41, midway through the second half, but Louisiana Tech ran off 12 straight points to take command.

Pam Thomas put the Lady Techsters up by 2 with 15.5 seconds left, and North Carolina brought the ball upcourt. With 4 seconds to play, Tonya Sampson took an off-balance shot and missed.

Tar Heel Marion Jones and Louisiana Tech's Kendra Neal fought for the loose ball. The whistle blew, and the referee signaled jump ball. The possession arrow belonged to UNC, keeping alive their faint hopes for victory.

Coach Hatchell called time-out and set up a play, a lob pass from inbounder Stephanie Lawrence to 6-foot, 5-inch center Sylvia Crawley. But Hatchell warned Lawrence to call another time-out if Crawley couldn't get open.

The Lady Techsters sensed the strategy and covered Crawley like glue. The Tar Heels signaled a second time-out.

Hatchell switched tactics. Two options, Sampson driving for a layup and Crawley setting for a jumper near the free-throw line would be decoys. North Carolina would go with a surprise play and try to win rather than send the game to overtime. Charlotte Smith would shoot a 3-pointer.

As the play unfolded, Sampson broke for the basket. As the coach had anticipated, Smith's defender slid away to double team Sampson. Lawrence whipped a pass to the unguarded Smith who stood just outside the 3-point arc.

Charlotte bent her knees slightly and lofted a high, soft floater. The buzzer sounded with the ball still rising. The sphere spun downward and swished through the hoop. The arena erupted as North Carolina won its first NCAA women's basketball championship, 60–59.

The decision to let Charlotte Smith shoot for the win seemed odd. During the season, Smith had connected only 8 of 31 times from 3-point range. But Hatchell counted on the unexpected and placed her faith in the unheralded star. Charlotte proved willing to try.

The coach was right. A relatively ordinary basketball player, Charlotte Smith, came through with an extraordinary shot to become an unlikely heroine.

Like the North Carolina coach, God often chooses ordinary people to accomplish extraordinary tasks for Him. He selected the reluctant Moses, a murderer with a speech problem, to lead the Israelites out of Egypt and slavery. He used the suffering and childless Hannah to provide the great priest Samuel.

Jesus named common fishermen and hated tax collectors as His disciples. The Lord chose Saul of Tarsus, a persecutor of Christians, to make missionary journeys, planting the Gospel throughout the world.

The Father anointed us to be His children and appointed us to be His heart, hands, and voice in the world. He asks that we be willing to put our ordinary selves under His control. Then He can accomplish extraordinary things through us.

Think about some ordinary people who have had extraordinary accomplishments in life. You may want to include Bible characters, athletes, and other well-known people in addition to women and men from your church or community. Make yourself available to God. Ask Him to accomplish extraordinary tasks through you.

MARATHON SWIMMER THIRSTS IN WATER

The poor and needy search for water, but there is none; their tongues are parched with thirst. But I the Lord will answer them; I, the God of Israel, will not forsake them. I will make rivers flow on barren heights, and springs within the valleys. I will turn the desert into pools of water, and the parched ground into springs. —ISAIAH 41:17-18

At age 16, Diana Nyad dreamed of landing a berth on the 1968 United States Olympic swimming team. But an infected heart valve quashed her plans.

The swimmer switched from speed to distance. Over the next 12 years, she completed an 8-hour journey around Manhattan Island and a 20-hour trek across Lake Ontario.

In August 1978, Nyad embarked on a 110-mile swim from Cuba to Key West. To avoid sharks, she labored inside a 20-foot by 40-foot steel cage suspended on pontoons. But Diana received no relief from the crushing waves, stinging jellyfish, or tongue-swelling saltwater.

After 12 hours in the water, the marathon swimmer experienced hallucinations, seeing spiders inside her cage. Acute seasickness set in, rendering Diana incapable of taking nourishment and leading to dehydration.

Despite her suffering, Nyad refused to quit. For 30 more hours, she battled the elements. Her support crew finally informed her that rough seas had blown the boat off course. Diana had swum 70 miles but completed only 50 of her intended route.

With no hope of completing her odyssey, the 29 year old reluctantly left the water. Soon after her recovery, Nyad plotted another ocean trek. A year later, Diana attempted a 60-mile swim from the Bahamas to Florida. But a man-of-war sting partially paralyzed her, and she abandoned the quest.

Nyad set out on the same route after a two-week layoff. On her

second try, the Florida native battled the tricky Gulf Stream, avoided sharks and jellyfish, and completed her improbable journey. Hundreds hugged and kissed her as Diana waded ashore following a 27-hour and 38-minute grueling swim.

Few people can fathom participating in any activity for more than several hours. After all, most workers spend just eight to ten hours on the job, and they take breaks every couple of hours. School days are even shorter.

Most people can't imagine swimming continuously for 42 hours or a day or part of a day or even for an hour. But Diana stayed in the water for hours upon hours. She chose to stroke toward her goal.

On the trip to Key West, she was thirsty but couldn't drink. She needed food but couldn't eat. The deadly tentacles of jellyfish stung welts on her body. The rolling seas brought waves of nausea. And yet she remained determined to continue. It was almost as if she thirsted for land and the completion of her swim.

People thirst for something more in life. We thirst for God. We need what He provides. We feel parched inside without the Lord's cooling moisture. We feel dry without His refreshing dew.

But the Heavenly Father promises us living water. He gives us rivers of love and springs of salvation. He provides refreshing pools of peace and joy. But we must choose to drink.

Go swimming if possible. Try to stay afloat as long as you can, aiming for at least 10 minutes. How long were you able to make it? Did being in the water make you thirsty? Drink a glass of icy, cool liquid. Praise God for the living water He provides.

RUNNER SEES WAY TO GOLD MEDAL

Saul got up from the ground, but when he opened his eyes he could see nothing. So they led him by the hand into Damascus. For three days he was blind, and did not eat or drink anything. —ACTS 9:8-9

At age nine, Marla Runyan realized she couldn't read the classroom blackboard. Then her vision rapidly faded. The Runyans visited eye specialist after eye specialist, but nothing helped. After two years, doctors finally diagnosed Marla's problem as Stargardt's Disease, an inherited disorder. The condition results in irreversible deterioration of the retina. Although incurable, the disease eventually stabilizes.

By age 14, Marla's vision had been reduced to 20/300, classifying her as legally blind. She could distinguish indistinct images on the periphery, but objects straight ahead appeared as a hazy clutter.

Runyan switched from soccer to track when poor eyesight left her unable to see the ball. At Camarillo, California's Adolfo High School, Marla high jumped 5' 7". Although the height set a school record, she attracted no attention from college coaches.

The former jumper enrolled as a regular student at San Diego State University and walked onto the track squad. For two years she competed only in her high school specialty.

A new head coach, Rahn Sheffield, convinced Marla to try the heptathlon. Without the ability to see clearly, Runyan learned to depend exclusively on timing and concentration in the competition that includes seven different events over a two-day period. She participated in the 100-meter hurdles, high jump, shot put, and the 200-meters on the first day. On the second day, she tried the long jump, javelin throw, and the 800-meter run. A table established by the International Amateur Athletic Federation determined points awarded for each performance.

After scoring 5,708 points and placing tenth in the 1996 Olympic heptathlon trials, the multi-talented athlete changed events once more, moving to the 1500 meters. She competed in the race for only the fifth time in the 1999 Pan American Games.

Canada's Leah Pells led after the first lap, but Marla believed her closing kick could overcome the frontrunner. As the competitors rounded the final curve, the 30 year old sensed Pells' fatigue and blazed down the stretch.

The gap narrowed as the pair simultaneously broke the tape. Photos showed that Runyan's torso crossed just ahead of her opponent. Although both recorded identical times of 4:16.86, Marla claimed the gold medal.

How did Marla Runyan win without the ability to see? In fact, how did she even run the race? She made up for her vision with her other senses. She felt the nearness of the other runners. She heard the pounding of feet on the ground and their heavy breathing. She set her internal clock to the curve of the track. She saw not with her eyes but with the rest of her being.

The Apostle Paul knew what it meant to be blind. The Lord scaled his eyes on the road to Damascus. God used Saul's blindness to open his eyes to the truth of Jesus' life, death, and resurrection. Paul received a new life and a new name.

God wants us to see the truth of His word. If we see only with our eyes, we miss the point. We must see beyond mere vision and see the truth with our hearts.

Do you know someone who is blind? If so, discuss how they want to be treated and how they have learned to cope with their lack of vision. Remember, they are blind, not deaf, so speak in a normal tone of voice. Praise God for the gift of sight. Ask Him to give you insight into His word and into the needs of others.

He also said, "This is what the kingdom of God is like. A man scatters seed on the ground. Night and day, whether he sleeps or gets up, the seed sprouts and grows, though he does not know how. All by itself the soil produces grain—first in the stalk, then the head, then the full kernel in the head. As soon as the grain is ripe, he puts the sickle to it, because the harvest has come." —MARK 4:26-29

Dot Richardson began her softball career in Orlando, Florida, with the Union Park Jets, a Class A Amateur Softball Association (ASA) fast-pitch team. At season's end, the 10 year old earned an All-Star team selection and prepared for a Tennessee tournament.

But while playing in her backyard, Dot slipped off an old automobile. She landed on a rusty sickle, slicing her foot. The wound required fifteen stitches to close.

Instead of going with her teammates to Tennessee, the aspiring softball player registered for an instructional league supervised by the Orlando Rebels. The Rebels, an ASA Major League team, gleaned prospects for their roster from the girls they taught.

At the league's conclusion, Dot joined the parent club as a bat girl. Although she spent much of her time picking up equipment, the 11 year old also played catch and shagged fly balls with women two and three times her age.

In the late summer of 1974, the Rebels led an Alabama team 10–0 in the top of the sixth. Since bat girls counted as official team members, manager Marge Ricker inserted Richardson into right field. In Dot's first at bat, she drove in a run with a single. Ricker signaled for a steal, and the preteen slid into second. The next batter hit safely, and Richardson motored home and beat the throw to score a run.

In the field, Dot caught a routine fly ball for out number one.

Later, an opposing batter flared a shallow liner to right. The rookie fielder scooped the ball and pegged a shot to first to end the game. Richardson's first appearance in the "majors" had been brief but memorable.

Another season in the instructional league followed. At its completion, Dot joined the Little Rebels, an ASA team for girls 15 and under. But a week later, Ricker pulled the 13 year old aside. The "adult" Rebels had decided to add Dot to their roster. Richardson became the youngest player in the history of ASA Women's Major League softball.

Thus the seeds were scattered to begin Dot Richardson's athletic career. She sprouted and grew through girls' and instructional leagues. But no one knew quite how she became full-grown in the game at 13.

The Floridian continued to reap the benefit of her sport, eventually playing for UCLA while completing pre-med studies. By 1996 at age 34, the orthopedic surgeon harvested a gold medal in the Atlanta Olympics, softball's first time in the competition. As part of Team U.S.A., she qualified four years later for the Sydney (Australia) Games.

The kingdom of God also sprouts, but from seeds of the Word scattered on the hearts and minds of people. And while those who sow the kernels may not understand the results, God provides the growth. Finally, the harvest yields the grain of new Christians.

Eat some whole grain bread or cereal. Think about the process that took the seed from planting to harvest to usable product. Think of some friends who don't know Christ. How could you plants the seeds of the kingdom of God in their lives? It may be a long process, but prayer and God's spirit will grow the seeds you plant.

INDIANA FARM GIRL LEADS ARKANSAS TO VICTORY

> *And Ruth the Moabitess said to Naomi, "Let me go to the fields and pick up the leftover grain behind anyone in whose eyes I find favor." Naomi said to her, "Go ahead, my daughter." So she went out and began to glean in the fields behind the harvesters. As it turned out, she found herself working in a field belonging to Boaz who was from the clan of Elimelech.*
>
> **—RUTH 2:2-3**

Christy Smith grew up surrounded by 15-foot high cornfields on a farm outside of Otterbein, Indiana. Her father, a former collegiate wrestler at Ball State, built a makeshift basketball court for his daughter's practice.

At Benton Central High School, the country girl lettered in basketball, swimming, volleyball, and track, winning the 800 meters at the Indiana state meet as a junior. On the court, she scored 1,082 points, grabbed 232 rebounds, made 506 assists, and totaled 418 steals.

Word of her skills reached Gary Blair, head coach at the University of Arkansas. When he first visited the Smith home and saw the court, the scene reminded him of the movie *Field of Dreams*.

Christy signed with the Lady Razorbacks and continued her success. The Hoosier state point guard played almost every minute of every game in her first year and won SEC Freshman of the Year honors.

Over the next three seasons, the four-year starter battled two knee injuries and numerous lacerations, bumps, and bruises. But Christy never slackened her efforts and forced Coach Blair to nearly drag her off the court.

Arkansas lost four of its final five games heading into the 1998 NCAA basketball tournament. Because of their lackluster record, the Lady Razorbacks received a ninth seed and a slot in the bracket with number one-ranked Stanford.

But Harvard upset Stanford, and Arkansas emerged victorious in the sub-regional. Coach Blair's squad faced a strong Kansas team in the west regional opener.

Down 32–38 at halftime, the Lady Razorbacks erupted for 51 second-half points to defeat the Jayhawks, 79–63. Christy scored 14 points and didn't commit a single turnover in her 39 minutes of action.

The regional final matched number two Duke against Arkansas. The game rocked back and forth until the final seconds.

With the Razorbacks leading 73–72, the Blue Devils fouled Christy with 31.7 seconds remaining. Following a time-out, the point guard hit her first free throw. Duke called another, but an unfazed Smith sank the second.

After Arkansas regained possession in the final seconds, a foul call sent Christy to the line once more. She calmly connected on both shots, and the Lady Razorbacks advanced to the Final Four for the first time with a 77–72 victory.

Christy Smith's life began on a farm. She honed her basketball skills in the Indiana grain fields. Her calmness under pressure was born of the quiet times in her country home. Her hard work came from long days of chores, working sunup until sundown.

In the Bible, Ruth made a new home in the fields near Bethlehem. As she picked up the leftover barley, working steadily from morning until night, she caught the eye of the harvesters. Then her calm spirit and hard work impressed the land owner. Boaz's kind words soothed her as she found protection in him. And he eventually chose her to be his wife.

Read the story of Ruth in the Bible. If possible, spend a quiet afternoon on a farm, helping with chores. What other things are achieved with steady, persistent work? Knitting a sweater, growing crops, and training for athletic prowess are just a few. Be steady and persistent in your study of God and His Word. It will produce amazing results!

Forget the former things; do not dwell on the past. See, I am doing a new thing! Now it springs up; do you not perceive it? I am making a way in the desert and streams in the wasteland. —ISAIAH 43:18-19

When Julie Harrington joined the professional tennis circuit in 1979 at age 16, the local Spokane newspaper described her as, "a neat package of fire, steel, and intense desire." But after 6 years of touring in obscurity, the 5-foot, 5-inch lefthander exchanged the courts of tennis for the courts of law.

Harrington experienced great joy but little financial reward during her playing days. The sights and smells of Wimbledon, Roland Garros, and Forest Hills remained vivid memories, but her career earnings totaled only $250,000.

Julie eventually rose to a number 35 world ranking. Her greatest triumph occurred during her first professional season in the 1979 U.S. Open. After 4 tough qualifying matches, the world's 126th best player faced Pam Shriver, the 1978 Open runner-up. Harrington defeated her 17th ranked opponent and won 2 more matches before being eliminated.

Retirement followed Julie's appearance in the 1984 Open. After losing in the first week, she flew to Seattle to take her admissions test to enter Gonzaga University. Harrington had never completed high school and qualified for college by passing an equivalency test.

The former tennis pro made the dean's list and graduated with a degree in political science and a minor in psychology. She then entered law school, completing her education in 1990. Several months later, Julie opened her own law practice, specializing in family law and estate planning.

Harrington struggled for five years to watch professional tennis on television. The game had consumed so much of her life for so long that she had difficulty enjoying it as a spectator.

But the 37-year-old attorney adjusted to life off the court and in the courtroom. Married to Rich Vela, she began teaching private tennis lessons and devoting most of her free time to their daughter, Brandi, born February 4, 1999.

Sometimes it's not easy to put the past behind and move forward. It was hard for Julie Harrington to give up tennis. But the time had come. She loved the game, but her moderate success convinced her she needed to get on with her education and her life. Yet God gave her new and wonderful things—a rewarding career in law, a family, tennis students, and the ability to enjoy her sport again on television.

God wants us to savor today and look forward to the time to come. Every day He provides new knowledge, new experiences, new direction, new opportunities, and new closeness. But we'll miss out if we keep thinking about what has been or what might have been. We can even lose the future He has planned if we dwell on the past.

What happens to a tennis player who continually thinks about the last shot or the last game or the last set or the last match? How much time does a track star lose when she sneaks a backward peek? What about the skater who looks back at what should have been a blind jump landing? Remember that in life too much looking back prevents moving forward. Praise God for the new things He does. Ask Him to help you let go of the past.

JUBILANT LIPINSKI CHALLENGES LYRICAL KWAN

Shout for joy to the Lord, all the earth, burst into jubilant song with music; make music to the Lord with the harp, with the harp and the sound of singing, with trumpets and the blast of the ram's horn—shout for joy before the Lord, the King. Let the sea resound, and all that is in it, the world, and all who live in it. Let the rivers clap their hands, let the mountains sing together for joy. —PSALM 98:4-8

Michelle Kwan arrived at the 1998 Nagano (Japan) Winter Olympics on the heels of an incredible achievement. A month earlier, the Californian had captured the United States Figure Skating Championship, earning 15-out-of-18 perfect 6.0s for artistry. But Tara Lipinski, the defending World Champion, relished her underdog role.

During the competition, Kwan elected to stay in a hotel with her family. However, the 15-year-old Lipinski savored the full sights and sounds of the Games by residing in the Olympic village.

In the short program, the newly crowned American titlist garnered 8-of-9 judges' votes for first place. But Tara remained convinced the free skate portion worth 2/3 of the scoring would be hers.

Because of the draw, Kwan skated first, choosing "Lyra Angelica" as her music. Perhaps due to the opening slot or the pre-competition hype, Michelle appeared deliberate and cautious rather than angelic.

In the early stages of her program, she wobbled out of a triple flip and landed a bit uncertainly on a triple loop. Although Kwan's confidence steadily increased as she skated, her technical marks suffered. They ranged from 5.7 to 5.8. Despite Michelle's across-the-board 5.9's for artistic merit, a strong, clean performance by Lipinski would challenge her for the gold.

Tara, performing in the fifth position to the music of "The Rainbow," grabbed the judges' attention immediately. The teenager completed 7 triple jumps, including her trademark triple loop-triple loop combination.

At the program's end, applause cascaded from the audience. Lipinski jubilantly bolted across the ice into the waiting arms of her coach and family.

Tara's impeccable maneuvers, coupled with a dazzling smile and upbeat tempo, garnered top scores from 6 of the 9 judges. The teen became the youngest Olympic figure skating gold medalist of all time, while Michelle Kwan settled for silver.

That evening Tara Lipinski shouted for joy. Throughout the games she had felt the jubilance of athletes from around the globe. She had listened to the music of a myriad of voices and felt her heart singing as she cheered teammates. She became not an individual competitor, but an integral part of the games. She blasted onto the ice with lyrics in her body and soul.

In the Bible, the psalmist felt the same jubilation. He shouted for joy and encouraged the earth to glorify God with trumpets, harp, clapping, and song. He asked all of us to praise the Lord with music in our bodies and souls.

As part of your time alone with God, sing a praise song or hymn. Clap your hands. Use an instrument if you play. Joyfully express your feelings about the Lord. Read Psalm 98 out loud as music to the King. Ask God to help you live and serve Him with jubilation.

TRACK OR BASKETBALL? WHICH CHOICE WAS BEST?

*For to me, to live is Christ and to die is gain. If I am
to go on living in the body, this will mean fruitful
labor for me. Yet what shall I choose? I do not know? I am torn
between the two: I desire to depart and be with Christ, which is
better by far; but it is more necessary for you that I remain in
the body.* —PHILIPPIANS 1:21-24

Sports fans wondered why Marion Jones opted for
collegiate basketball over track and field. But after her
North Carolina Tar Heels defeated Louisiana Tech for the 1994
NCAA basketball crown, no one doubted her reasoning. Jones
described the feeling as one that could never be matched.

But Marion changed direction again and caused people to shake
their heads. After winning one national and three conference
championships, the third-team All-American point guard
switched back to track.

Despite missing the 1996 Atlanta Olympics due to a fractured
foot, the Los Angeles native quickly rose to sprinting's top ranks.
At the 1997 U.S. Track and Field Championships, Jones claimed
double golds in the 100 meters and long jump. Two months later,
she took first place in the World Championship 100 meters.

The 1998 Goodwill Games billed the 100-meter race as "The
Women of Speed." Every competitor possessed a personal best of
under 11 seconds, and all three 1996 Olympic medalists, Gail
Devers—gold, Merlene Ottey—silver, and Gwen Torrence—
bronze, entered.

The race lost a bit of glitter when nagging ailments forced
Devers and Torrence to withdraw, but a fleet field nonetheless
prepared to run. Marion blew everyone away, setting a new meet
record of 10.90 seconds.

The 200-meter event scripted almost identically. Jones challenged the world's fastest and defeated them all by more than 0.5

seconds. She established a new Goodwill Games mark of 21.80 seconds.

During the 1998 track season, the phenomenal runner captured first place in 35 of 36 competitions. Marion would approach the 2000 Sydney (Australia) Olympics with aspirations of winning five gold medals. Many believed this opportunity would determine whether or not she would become the heir to great American Olympic sprinters such as Florence Griffith Joyner and Jackie Joyner Kersee.

Marion Jones had a choice to make when she graduated from high school. Would she run track or play basketball? The star athlete probably couldn't lose with either decision. She opted for basketball, a wise move for her teammates and confirmed when she earned a championship ring. And then she discovered she could try track again even though she was out of running form and shape, again a successful selection proved by gold medals.

In his letter to the Philippians in the Bible, Paul discussed a choice in his life. He knew he neared death and everlasting life with God. He longed for eternity in the Father's presence. Yet he believed others would profit more from his continuing instruction and service.

Paul felt torn, just as we often feel torn when we must decide between two equally attractive options. His choice came down to what was best for growing Christians, though not necessarily for himself. God asks us to be true to ourselves but to consider others when making choices.

If you had been Marion Jones, what decision would you have made? Why? Consider a choice you made between two good options. Looking back, would you have made a different selection? Ask God to help you make the best choices in life.

WOMEN'S PROFESSIONAL BASKETBALL LEAGUE STARTS AND FINISHES

"All this is in writing," David said, "because the hand of the Lord was upon me, and he gave me understanding in all the details of the plan." David also said to Solomon his son, "Be strong and courageous, and do the work. Do not be afraid or discouraged, for the Lord God, my God is with you. He will not fail you or forsake you until all the work for the service of the temple of the Lord is finished." —1 CHRONICLES 28:19-20

In 1978, Bill Byrne believed the time had arrived for professional women's basketball. He banked on the 1980 Olympics to provide a nucleus of media stars for his new creation, the Women's Professional Basketball League. Unfortunately, not enough money and a United States Olympic boycott turned an idealistic notion into a struggle of impoverished owners, frustrated coaches, and underpaid players.

The League opened in 1979 with eight teams playing a 34-game schedule. But the four best-known court stars shunned the new enterprise. Carol Blazejowski and Ann Myers retained their amateur status for future eligibility. Lusia Harris earned more money as a Delta State University admissions counselor, and Nancy Lieberman had two years of college eligibility remaining at Old Dominion.

The players endured incredible hardships and made immense sacrifices. In the middle of winter after playing the Chicago Hustle, the Iowa Cornets boarded a bus and crept six hours through snow to engage the Minnesota Fillies. The team played in sweaty, dirty uniforms thawed after they froze in the luggage compartment.

The WPBL's inaugural season ended on an upbeat note as the Houston Angels defeated the Cornets for the championship before nearly 6,000 fans. *Sports Illustrated* described the first year as, "red ink, rosy future."

But the situation worsened and never improved. The League's

second year witnessed failed franchises, coaching resignations, pathetic attendance, and undercurrents of dissension. The New York Stars emerged as the second-year champions over the Cornets.

Unbelievably, the WPBL existed for a third year. The League's lowest point occurred on March 22, 1982. Before their game with the St. Louis Streak, the Minnesota Fillies' entire squad quit in a dispute over late paychecks. Owner Gordon Nevers quickly assembled a pick-up roster of six free agents and three college seniors but lost 128–80.

The Nebraska Wranglers edged the Dallas Diamonds for the final crown. Diamonds owner David Almstead tried to revive the WPBL but garnered no support. After three attempted meetings, Almstead announced the once promising League had died.

Bill Byrne dreamed a dream and developed a plan. He displayed great courage. He worked hard to build a league. But the time for professional women's basketball had not yet come. It would be nearly two decades before the idea would find success.

In the Bible, King David had a plan. God had given him details for building the temple. But the time had not come. The Lord wanted David's son Solomon to complete the project.

While David desired to see the temple finished, he knew that was not God's will. And the king accepted God's plan. David assured his child that God would guide him until the work was done.

Sometimes God gives us great plans, but the time has not yet come. Though difficult, we must be willing to lay the groundwork, accept God's timetable, and support His choice for accomplishing the dream.

Read in an encyclopedia or on the internet about the building and remodeling projects of the White House, home to the United States President's family. Notice how many times those who planned and worked were not able to enjoy the beautiful residence. Thank God for the plans He gives. Ask Him for understanding when He chooses others to complete them.

GOLFER FOLLOWS FATHER'S ADVICE TO PRO TOUR

And I will put my Spirit in you and move you to follow my decrees and be careful to keep my laws.

—EZEKIEL 36:27

Jacqueline "Jackie" Liwai learned golf as a child. At age 7, she caddied for her father, captain of the Hawaii Golf Club. The young girl judiciously followed his advice to "Be quiet, watch, and learn."

The young Hawaiian woman never dreamed the game could become her vocation. At various times she worked as an Army payroll clerk, waitress, taxi driver, and Sears Roebuck sales clerk before embarking on the professional golf circuit.

Married and with two young daughters, Jackie Pung borrowed enough money to enter the 1952 United States Women's Amateur in Oregon. Her surprise victory left the 30 year old in a quandary. She could return to Hawaii and her family, or she could join the newly formed Ladies Professional Golf Association Tour.

Pung opted for her childhood sport, leaving her husband and daughters for months at a time. Although she loved the competition and camaraderie, golf brought Jackie little money.

In 1957, Jackie's career instantly reversed from tribulation to jubilation and back again. At the United States Women's Open, the 35-year-old golfer sank a 6-foot putt on the 72nd hole to card a 298, edging the great Betsy Rawls for first place by 1 stroke. She triumphantly hugged her 15-year-old daughter Barnette.

Moments later, United States Golf Association Executive Director, Joseph Dey, interrupted the apparent champion during a telephone interview. Inspection of Jackie's scorecard revealed an error.

Her playing partner, Betty Jameson, had marked a 5 rather than Pung's correct score, a 6, on hole number four. In her excitement, the Hawaiian signed her card without checking the individual hole-by-hole scores. But golf's rigid rules allow no compromise. A player who reports a lower than actual score receives automatic disqualification.

Although members of the Winged Foot Golf Club took up a $3,000 collection to offset her lost winnings, the ruling stunned Jackie. She retreated to Manhattan's Lexington Hotel and didn't touch a club for three weeks.

Pung ultimately returned to the LPGA tour, but lack of tournament victories led to her 1964 retirement. However, she still used the game as her vocation. She returned to Hawaii as an instructor, and in 1976, Jackie received the LPGA Teacher of the Year award.

Jackie's daddy instilled in her his spirited love of golf. But when he let his daughter on the course as his caddy, he insisted she follow his rules. She needed to listen. She needed to know the clubs. She needed to discover how to play the ball from different lies.

But more than her father's instructions, she also needed to understand the rules of the game. Jackie learned them, but that one day in her excitement she forgot. She wasn't careful. She made a mistake. And she paid the price.

The Prophet Ezekiel reminds us that when we follow God, He instills His Spirit inside us. The Heavenly Father then expects us to follow His rules. But sometimes we don't listen. In our excitement or hurry, we forget. We aren't careful. We make a mistake. And we pay the price.

If you're not familiar with them, review some of golf's rules. Why do you think they're so inflexible? Read God's laws in Exodus 20:1-17. Why do you think God's rules are so rigid? Ask the Heavenly Father to help you follow His commands.

Everyone who quotes proverbs will quote this proverb about you: "Like mother, like daughter." —EZEKIEL 16:44

Patricia "Pat" Keller missed making the 1948 United States Olympic diving team by less than .01 point. Rather than quit, the 17 year old challenged herself to claim the gold next time.

The young woman who spent her childhood days on Santa Monica's Muscle Beach endured countless abrasions, lacerations, and contusions to perfect her acrobatic art. In 1950, Pat Keller McCormick won both the 1-meter and 3-meter springboards plus the two-story platform at the National AAU diving championships.

Two years and thousands of dives later, the Californian traveled to Helsinki, Finland, for the 1952 Olympic games. In the springboard competition, she bettered France's Madeleine Moreau for first place. Later in the platform event, Pat topped fellow Americans Paula Jean Meyers and Juno Irwin Stover for her second gold.

But her double victory didn't bring immediate acclaim. When McCormick returned home, a neighbor inquired if she had been on vacation.

In 1955, Pat became pregnant with her and Glenn's first child. Despite the inconvenience, she trained and swam half a mile until two days before the boy's birth. McCormick returned to Olympic competition in 1956. At the Melbourne games, the mother of an eight-month-old son repeated her double golds in the springboard and platform, making her the rare recipient of a "double-double."

In recognition of her outstanding athletic achievements, *Sports Illustrated* named Pat "Athlete of the Year," and the Associated Press and United Press International both selected her as "Woman

of the Year." The four-time gold medal diver garnered the 1956 Sullivan Award as the nation's top amateur athlete.

At the 1984 Los Angeles games, another diving McCormick splashed on the Olympic scene. Kelly, Pat's 24-year-old daughter, captured the silver in the springboard competition, missing gold by fewer than 4 points.

Like her mother, the younger McCormick participated and medaled in back-to-back Olympiads. In the 1988 Seoul (Korea) games, she claimed a springboard bronze. Pat and Kelly represent the only mother-daughter medalists in Olympic history.

As a child, Kelly saw her mother's medals. She aspired to become a winning Olympic diver just like her mom. But while Pat took pride in her daughter following in her footsteps, she made it clear her love was not dependent on athletic achievement. It was unconditional. And Kelly's teammates remembered her as much for her sensitive friendship as for her high dives.

Like Pat, like Kelly. Like mother, like daughter. The Bible explains that when a mother sets a positive example and teaches her little girl to love God and His ways, she usually will. On the other hand, Ezekiel states that when mothers become arrogant, unconcerned, haughty, do detestable things before God, and do not help the poor and needy, they will likely pass those same traits to their daughters.

In His kingdom, God desires godly mothers who produce daughters who equal or surpass them.

Think about some mothers and daughters you know who prove "like mother, like daughter" true. In what ways are you like your mother? Have you tried to emulate her? Or have you tried not to? Thank the Heavenly Father for godly mothers. If your mother is alive and has set a positive example for you, give her a call or write to tell her so.

TENNIS STARS ENGAGE IN BATTLE OF WORDS

Whatever exists has already been named, and what man is has been known; no man can contend with one who is stronger than he. The more the words, the less the meaning, and how does that profit anyone? —ECCLESIASTES 6:10-11

Bobby Riggs, the 1939 Wimbledon and United States tennis champion, engaged Margaret Court in a promotional exhibition on Mother's Day 1973. The 55-year-old hustler claimed women tennis professionals couldn't defeat even, "an old man with one foot in the grave." Court fell victim to the hype, Riggs' words, and his assortment of junk shots. She lost the winner-take-all match, 6–2, 6–1.

The farce infuriated Billy Jean King. She challenged Bobby to another match which the press quickly dubbed, "The Battle of the Sexes."

Houston's Astrodome hosted the exhibition on September 20, 1973. More than 30,000 spectators witnessed the event live. An estimated 50 million watched on prime time television.

For Riggs, the contest merely represented a chance to grab the spotlight and perhaps a big paycheck. But to King, the made-for-television spectacle represented the opportunity of a lifetime.

Winning would enhance both women athletes' image and marketability. In the locker room prior to warm-ups, Billy Jean resolved she would emerge victorious.

Both participants attempted to "out-psych" the other. They pulled out all theatrical stops and engaged in a battle of words. Riggs entered the arena in a Chinese rickshaw pulled by beautiful females. Bare-chested males carried King to the court on a feathered Egyptian litter.

Following wordy pre-match introductions and promotions, the pair finally began to play. King, the 29-year-old underdog, took command from the outset. Her strong serves and consistent volleys forced Riggs to run the baseline. His aging legs grew tired. In spite of his boasts that no woman could defeat him, he struggled against Billy Jean.

The 1973 women's Wimbledon titlist captured the match and the $100,000 purse in straight sets, 6–4, 6–3, 6–3. After the final point, King flung her racket toward the rafters as Riggs jumped the net to shake her hand.

In the end, all the words and all the hype didn't matter. Performance did. In spite of what he said, Bobby Riggs could not contend with Billy Jean King's training, agility, and strength.

Words are important in life. They can soothe or persuade. They help establish friendships and communicate love. But if words aren't backed by actions and strength of character, they become worthless.

Too often we talk about being good Christians. We make the right comments about prayer, Bible study, and worship. We quote the ten commandments. We say we love our neighbors as ourselves.

But God doesn't like just talk. He wants us to pray, read His Bible, and worship. He requires us to obey His commandments. He expects us to show love for our neighbors. He wants us to live our faith.

The Lord desires that we put our words into action.

Observe coaches and athletes in media interviews. Note how many of them say they're great but don't live up to their words. Ask God to help you live a Christian life, not just talk about it.

To all perfection I see a limit; but your commands are boundless. —PSALM 119:96

Athletes strive to achieve consistent performance. At times, their skills seem nearly perfect. On other occasions, untimely injuries completely bind and hobble them.

In December 1996, the George Mason University Patriots played in the Central Florida University Tournament. The Patriots advanced by defeating Western Michigan, 68–63. In the semifinals, the George Mason women took on the host school.

Before a paltry crowd of 175, the Fairfax, Virginia, team battled to a 40–30 halftime lead. But the Patriots erupted in the second half with point guard Kristeena Alexander leading the way.

Although the Hempstead, New York, freshman and high school teammate of Chamique Holdsclaw at Christ the King hit only 4 of 10 shots from the field, her free throws proved amazing. Kristeena hit 20 of 20 to pace George Mason with 28 points. Krista Jay added 21, and Taisha Thomas netted 12 to aid in the 82–65 victory over the Golden Knights.

Alexander's performance put her at the top of the NCAA Division I record book. Four players had previously canned 18 of 18.

The following night in the finals against number 10 ranked Auburn, the Patriots trailed the entire contest. But the fabulous freshman nailed a last-second shot, sending the game into overtime.

Thomas scored 7 points in the extra period, and Maria Acevedo converted 2 clutch free throws in the final moments to seal the 58–55 upset win. Kristeena garnered 3 steals during overtime to spark the Patriot victory.

At season's end, Alexander received the Colonial Athletic Association Rookie of the Year award and earned a tryout with the

United States Junior National team. But her fortunes quickly reversed.

During the summer of 1997, Kristeena underwent ankle surgery to repair torn cartilage. Following a frustrating fall semester, she left George Mason and enrolled at George Washington University.

As required by NCAA regulations, Alexander sat out the 1997-98 season. The point guard returned to competition for George Washington in December 1998. At the season's conclusion, she won an award at her new university when named the Colonials' Newcomer of the Year.

Kristeena Alexander played outstanding basketball. She always shot free throws well. But on that one night, she was perfect. Twenty times she went to the charity stripe. Twenty times the ball swished through the hoop.

But the player's perfection had limits. The next night she shot the game-tying basket, but she wasn't perfect. She earned Rookie of the Year honors but found her potential athletic greatness bound by injury. Alexander initially felt success at George Mason but left in frustration. She rebounded at George Washington but won an award typically given to freshmen.

Life brings ups and downs. We are not perfect though we may have days when it seems we are. Our physical, mental, social, and spiritual ideals face limits.

But God has no such limits. He alone is perfect. His words, His care, and His love cannot be bound on earth or in heaven.

Remember the best athletic contest you ever played. Were you perfect? If so, were you perfect the next time? Think about the best day you ever lived. Was it perfect? If so, was the next day the same? Praise God for His perfection. Ask Him to help you understand your limits and live with your frustrations.

BORDERS SPARKLES ON DIAMOND

I made you grow like a plant of the field. You grew up and developed and became the most beautiful of jewels. —EZEKIEL 16:7

At an early age, Phil Borders found the key to his daughter's happiness. Ila didn't desire clothes or toys or special trips. The young girl only wanted a jewel, not a bit of crystallized carbon but the baseball field's green diamond.

The La Mirada, California, native began with softball. But after a trip to Dodger Stadium, the 10-year-old girl switched to the national pastime—baseball.

Ila Borders worked her way up through the La Miranda Little Leagues. A natural athlete, she could hit, throw, and run equally well. In spite of her success, observers remained skeptical of her advancement to higher levels of the sport.

The Borders enrolled their daughter in Whittier Christian High School to avoid a court fight with the public schools over Ila's right to play the boys' game. The Little League veteran made varsity as a freshman. On weekends, both father and daughter played on the same semi-pro squad.

After her junior year, the pitcher accepted a scholarship from Southern California College, the first offer ever granted a female baseball player. Confident in her abilities, Ila concluded her high school career by winning the team's Most Valuable Player award as a senior.

The collegiate hurler's first two years went smoothly, but a coaching change in year three brought turmoil and dissatisfaction. The pioneer pitcher transferred to Whittier College to play a final season.

On May 29, 1997, Barry Moss and Marty Scott of the Northern League's St. Paul Saints signed Ila to a professional contract. Two days later she became the first woman to pitch in professional baseball.

Shortly afterward, the Saints traded Borders to the Duluth-Superior Dukes. On July 9, 1998, Borders started her first professional baseball game and 15 days later collected her first victory.

From the time she was a tiny child, Ila Borders dreamed of starring on the field. Her father worked daily to help her obtain the necessary skills. The two spent hours catching fly balls, fielding grounders, batting, running bases, and pitching. With athletic ability given by the Heavenly Father and support and time provided by her earthly father, the girl grew and developed to become a beautiful jewel on the baseball diamond.

Fortunately others recognized Ila's talent and allowed her to successfully compete in the male sport.

God gives babies the ability to grow just like plants and flowers and trees. When nurtured and allowed to develop through the love of Christian fathers and mothers, children mature into something special. They sparkle like diamonds and other precious jewels with the light of the Heavenly Father reflected in them.

Examine the abilities and talents your Heavenly Father has given you. Consider how your earthly father or mother has helped nurture and develop them. Write a love note to one of your parents or to someone who has been like a mother or father to you. Praise God for Christian moms and dads.

Oh that my words were recorded, that they were written on a scroll, that they were inscribed within an iron tool on lead, or engraved in rock forever! I know that my Redeemer lives, and that in the end he will stand upon the earth.

—JOB 19:23-25

In high school LaTasha Jenkins dreamed of becoming a college professor. She intended to enroll at Tennessee State, but her parents convinced her to attend David Letterman's alma mater, Ball State, on a track scholarship.

In addition to her running, LaTasha remained true to her heart's calling and majored in English. She loved to write. When away from the track or classroom, she composed poetry, short stories, and narratives, letting her imagination run free. The young woman drew inspiration from Emily Dickinson and Toni Morrison.

But the Calumet Park, Illinois, native's feet also ran free. As a freshman, Jenkins won the Mid-American Conference (MAC) title in the 200 meters. In four years of competition, she won the event every time, only the second woman in MAC history to accomplish the feat.

At the 1998 NCAA Championship Track Meet, LaTasha finished second in the 200 meters to Georgia's Debbie Ferguson. In 1999 as a returning champion, Debbie drew the nod as the race favorite.

The gun sounded, and University of Texas star Nanceen Perry rushed to the early lead. But in the last 60 meters, Jenkins blasted to the front, passing every runner including Ferguson.

At the tape, LaTasha clocked a winning 22.29, her personal best and the second fastest time ever recorded by an American collegian. Ferguson closed strong to place second but lagged behind the champion by over 0.3 seconds. Tennessee's Kelli White nipped Perry for third.

Ball State sprinter coach Kelly Lycan marveled at the way the race unfolded. Seldom has a runner defeated a top-ranked field by such a large margin. Jenkins' blazing closing kick caused the crowd to ooh and aah.

But the gold medalist downplayed her accomplishment. She observed that earning track fame might create future demand for her writings.

LaTasha Jenkins loves running, and she loves writing. She enjoys the feel of the wind in her face as she races down the track, but she also enjoys the feel of her words racing across blank paper. She likes to read the accomplishments of Ball State's great runners on the sports page, and she likes to read the poetry and novels of the world's great writers.

LaTasha's running career will only last a few years. Her name will remain in the record book only until someone bests her marks. But her writing career can last a lifetime, and her name will remain with her works as long as people read them.

In the Old Testament, Job knew the value of the written word. He wanted the thoughts he penned to remain forever engraved in rock. What the suffering man learned might not be found on a scroll or stone, but it remains in the Bible and inscribed on the hearts of many Christians.

"I know that my Redeemer lives, and that in the end he will stand upon the earth" (Job 19:15).

If you can find a recording, listen to "I Know that My Redeemer Liveth" from Handel's great work, The Messiah. Think about the meaning. Consider poems and books you have read. Which do you think will last? Thank God for the Bible. Write Job 19:25 on your heart by memorizing its words.

"With bitterness archers attacked him [Joseph]; they shot at him with hostility. But his bow remained steady, his strong arms stayed limber, because of the hand of the Mighty One of Jacob, because of the Shepherd, the Rock of Israel." —GENESIS 49:23-24

Don Rabska has coached many top-flight archery students. But when actress Geena Davis approached him about taking lessons, he didn't know exactly what to expect.

The 1988 Academy-Award winner met her coach for the first time at a West Los Angeles private park in March 1997. Geena showed up alone dressed in workout clothes. She announced she wanted to train for the Olympics.

Davis had undergone FBI pistol training to prepare for the filming of *The Long Kiss Goodnight* in 1996. Instructors marveled at her natural shooting talent. She developed an interest in archery after watching American Justin Huish win two gold medals in the 1996 Atlanta games.

The star of *The Accidental Tourist* and *A League of Their Own* practiced intently. Over the next two years, she shot 300 arrows every day, 6 days a week, with her 70-inch carbon-and-aluminum recurve bow. Geena conditioned with weights and cardiovascular training.

The actress amazed fellow archers with her rapid progress. Most competitors take up the sport as children. Adults rarely master the bow in such a short time.

But the Boston University graduate qualified for the 1999 National Championships in Oxford, Ohio. She placed 29th out of 300 competitors and advanced to the United States Olympic semifinal try-outs in Bloomfield, New Jersey.

After learning of Geena's entry, reporters and movie fans descended on the small suburban park creating considerable distraction. In addition to the media attention, light rain hampered the novice archer's shooting. In a sport where steadiness and concentration separate winners from losers, she placed 24th in the field of 28 but vowed to seek an Olympic berth in four more years.

Geena Davis became fascinated by archery. She found the sport satisfying. Her steady hand and discerning eye made her a natural. She shot arrow after arrow aiming for the bulls-eye. Geena often scored the 10 points earned by hitting the small gold circle.

But prehistoric people didn't use their bows and arrows to hit targets. They hunted with the tool. Ancient Egyptians expanded the weapon for war. Today most archers shoot at targets though a few hunt with their bows. Children and youth enjoy the sport at summer camps.

The Bible mentions bows and arrows. In Genesis, Jacob included the weapon in the blessing he gave his son Joseph. The father likened Joseph's difficulties to an attack by archers. Then he compared God's gift of strength and steadiness to Joseph successfully shooting his bow.

The Heavenly Father also wants us to live our lives with steadiness and concentration on Him. Only then can we withstand the attacks of those who value evil over God.

If there's an archery range nearby, spend some time target shooting. Here are some archery tips that also apply to the Christian life:
- *You must keep your eye on the target.*
- *You must focus and not be distracted by the crowd.*
- *You must keep a steady hand and not waver from what is right.*
Praise God for the strength He gives. Ask the Lord to help you concentrate on Him.

At that time the disciples came to Jesus and asked, "Who is the greatest in the kingdom of heaven?" He called a little child and had him stand among them. And he said: "I tell you the truth, unless you change and become like little children, you will never enter the kingdom of heaven. Therefore, whoever humbles himself like this child is the greatest in the kingdom of heaven." —MATTHEW 18:1-4

The National Collegiate Athletic Association (NCAA) lagged in recognizing women's sports. Despite the 1972 passage of Title IX granting gender equity, almost a decade lapsed before the organization changed its thinking and took over women's programs. Until the early 1980s, the Association of Intercollegiate Athletics for Women (AIAW) governed female events.

During the transition, several small colleges developed powerhouse basketball programs. Immaculata, Delta State, and Old Dominion captured AIAW national titles. In 1974, athletic administrators at Louisiana Tech decided to change their focus and begin women's basketball. They assigned Sonja Hogg, former Ruston High School physical education teacher and coach, to develop the program.

Sonja relished the duty and worked relentlessly. She led the Lady Techsters to their first AIAW final four in 1979, losing the title to Old Dominion. The following year Louisiana Tech returned but fell once again to the Lady Monarchs in the semifinals.

Rolling to a 32–0 record in the 1980–81 season, Coach Hogg took her team to the finals for the third time. It proved the charm as the Lady Techsters defeated Tennessee, 79–59, to claim their first AIAW championship.

But change arrived the following year. The NCAA brought women's basketball under its umbrella, leaving the AIAW behind.

Sporting a 34–1 mark and a number-one national ranking, Hogg's team faced number two Cheyney State in the first NCAA finals. In the opening minutes, Coach Vivian Stringer's team confused the Louisiana players with a multiple zone defense. The Wolves jumped to a 20–14 lead midway through the first half.

Louisiana Tech called time-out, and Hogg substituted Debra Rodman for Pam Kelly to get better offensive rebounding. She also switched to a pressing, man-to-man defense to create turnovers and generate transition baskets. The Lady Techsters caught fire. They outscored Cheyney State, 26–4, over the last 9 minutes of the first half as the Wolves missed 13 of 15 shots.

Freshman forward Janice Lawrence scored 12 of her 20 points during the final minutes of the first half and received the game's MVP award. Louisiana Tech easily captured its second consecutive national title and the very first NCAA championship, 76–62.

During Hogg's tenure with the Lady Techsters, the program made 6 consecutive Final Four appearances. They earned national records for most wins in a season at 40 and consecutive victories at 54. Five players earned All-American honors and several won Olympic medals. The gym crowds moved from sit-wherever-you-want to standing-room-only.

Sonja Hogg and Louisiana Tech adapted to a new day in women's sports. They first began a basketball program then changed it to a winning one. And the Lady Techsters won that first NCAA championship by shifting players and defenses.

Jesus spoke of the need to change and the difference it can make. When His disciples asked who was greatest in the kingdom of heaven, the Lord answered that we have to become as little children to enter His kingdom. Then to be great, we must shift from pride to humility before the Father.

How hard is it for you to put aside pride? How much difficulty do you have passing to a teammate rather than taking the shot yourself? Do you mind specializing in defense, or do you long for the spotlight of scoring? Ask God to help you humble yourself. Praise Him for the gift of changed lives through faith in Jesus.

So Joseph also went up from the town of Nazareth in Galilee to Judea, to Bethlehem the town of David, because he belonged to the house and line of David. He went there to register with Mary, who was pledged to be married to him and was expecting a child. While they were there, the time came for the baby to be born, and she gave birth to her firstborn, a son. She wrapped him in strips of cloth and placed him in a manger, because there was no room for them in the inn.

—LUKE 2:4-7

Hours after her high school graduation, Dorothy "Dot" Richardson flew from her Orlando, Florida, home to Colorado Springs, Colorado, to try out for the U.S.A. softball squad. Although few considered the 17 year old a prospect for the 1979 Pan American competition, her surprise selection brought Dot great honor. But making the grade as a top American player meant years of travel ahead.

Richardson journeyed to Puerto Rico for her first international competition. That fall she enrolled at Western Illinois University but a year later transferred across the country to the University of California at Los Angeles (UCLA). After receiving her degree in kinesiology, Dot attended the University of Louisville Medical School. She moved back for an orthopedic surgical residency at the Los Angeles County/University of Southern California Medical Center.

As a collegian, medical school student, and surgical resident, the shortstop trekked around the world to compete. Studies, softball, and medicine left Dot little time for family and friends.

But when the holidays came each year, Dot never failed to fly back to her parents' Orlando home, usually arriving on Christmas Eve. Richardson often used her short holidays to squeeze in long postponed projects. During one Christmas break, the All-

American rallied her family and filmed two instructional softball videos at Union Park, her first field. Carols chiming from a nearby church could be heard faintly in the background.

Dr. Richardson established the tradition of hurriedly shopping on Christmas Eve for her father, mother, sister Kathy, brothers Kenny and Lonnie, and grandparents. Years added ten nieces and nephews to the growing list. But whatever she purchased, Dot remembered that it's the thought and the time together, not the cost, that's most valuable.

Though short, the hours spent with family celebrating Christ's birth always revived and sustained the busy physician-athlete. One holiday she and her grandfather found themselves riding alone together. Her beloved grandpa didn't look well and had difficulty breathing. In the car he shared about his wonderful life and his faith in God. Dot felt surrounded by the glow of Christmas and the glow of his love.

Her grandfather died a few weeks later. But Dot knew they would be together again one day in heaven. She believed it because of Jesus, the gift God gave at Christmas time.

And that's what God wants us to celebrate each holiday season, the gift of His Son.

Read the Christmas story in Luke 2. Sing or listen to your favorite carols and songs. Recall your most memorable holiday. What made it special? Begin to makes plans for the coming Christmas. Where will you be? Who will be there? What gifts will you give? Will the presents be marked more by meaning than money? Remember, that's what God wants. Praise the Heavenly Father for His gift of baby Jesus and for Mary and Joseph. Thank God for your family. Ask the Lord to bless your Christmas celebration.

GLOSSARY

MVP: Most Valuable Player, the highest award given in many sports.

NCAA: National Collegiate Athletic Association, the governing body for collegiate sports.

BASKETBALL

Assist: A pass that results in a basket.

Foul: Illegal contact by an opposing player.

Free throw: A free shot from the foul line by a player who has been fouled. It is also called a foul shot.

Hook shot: A high-arcing shot, using a sweeping motion.

Jump shot: A shot taken from medium to long range at the top of a jump. The jump allows the shooter to free herself from the defender and gives the shot more power.

Post: The area where the center usually sets up on offense, with her back to the basket.

Rebound: A retrieval of the ball as it bounces off the backboard or rim after an unsuccessful shot.

Tip-in: A field goal made by tipping a rebound into the basket.

FIGURE SKATING

Axel: The most difficult jump in figure skating named for its inventor Axel Paulson, a Norwegian speed skating champion from the early 1900s. Executing the Axel jump, a skater takes off from the inside edge while skating forward, turns one time in the air (540 degrees), and lands on the back outside edge of the other skate. A double Axel has 900 degrees, and a triple has 1,260 degrees.

Camel spin: Sometimes called the "parallel spin," the skater performs the camel with one leg lifted parallel to the ice. The name reflects the humped position often displayed by novices when learning the move.

Figures: A series of patterns based on the figure eight or three-circle serpentine form, sometimes called compulsories. There are 42 figures classified by the International Skating Union. The skater traces the pattern on clean ice three times. Performed well, the tracings will be virtually identical. In 1991, figures were eliminated from international competition after 100 years.

Loop jump: This jump is performed without a toe pick assist and is an edge jump in which the skater completes a loop in the air (or two or three), taking off from a backward outside edge and landing on the same back outside edge.

Lutz jump: A jump named for its inventor Alois Lutz. Moving backward on an outside edge, the skater picks in the toe of the opposite skate to assist the lift, makes one or more 360-degree rotations in a counter-rotational direction. The required counter-rotation means that the revolution is against the normal rotation direction, i.e. taking off on the right foot, normal rotation would be counterclockwise. In the Lutz, rotation would be clockwise. The jump can be anticipated by viewers as the skater gathers speed and slides backward in a large arc while glancing over her shoulder.

Salchow jump: A move developed by and named for the Swedish champion, Ulrich Salchow. The jump involves one or more complete midair turns from the back inside edge of one skate to back outside edge of the other skate. If done with a toe assist, the jump is called a toe Salchow or a flip jump.

Spin: A freestyle technique in which the skater revolves rapidly on her own axis in one spot on one foot. In competition, all spins must include at least six rotations. Spins may performed in many positions with some named for body position during the spin, such as sit spin, layback spin, or cross-foot spin.

Split jump: A flashy move in which the skater jumps into the air and performs a split in mid-air with the hand touching the ankles or toes. The jump is sometimes called a "Russian Split." When a half-revolution is added after touching the toes, the move is referred as a "Split Flip."

Toe loop: Also called the "cherry flip," the move is the easiest jump to master. The skater takes off from a back outside edge, picks the toes of her other skate into the ice to achieve height and does one 360 degree turn, or move, in the air, landing on the back inside edge of the takeoff skate.

GOLF

Birdie: A score of 1-under-par for a hole.

Bogey: A score of 1-over-par for a hole.

Chip: A short, lofted stroke used in approaching the green.

Drive: A golfer's first shot off the tee.

Eagle: A score of 2-under-par for a hole.

Green: The smooth grass area around each hole.

Hole-in-one: A golfer's drive that goes into the hole.

Par: The accepted number of strokes a good player should need when hitting the ball from the tee into the hole.

Putt: A short stroke used on the green to roll the ball into the hole.

Tee: A small peg that balances the ball just above the ground.

GYMNASTICS

Balance beam: A board 15 feet long, 4 inches high, and 4 inches wide on which gymnasts perform. This bar rests on supports and is 4 feet off the ground.

Floor exercise: A gymnastic routine performed on a 40-foot by 40-foot mat.

Uneven bars: Two wooden bars connected by cables or wooden poles. One bar is 7 feet, 9 inches tall, the other is 5 feet, 2 inches.

Vault: A padded piece of equipment 5 feet long, 4 feet high, and 14 inches wide over which gymnasts leap.

HOCKEY

Assist: Passing to a player who scores a goal.

Bodychecking: Using the body to bump an opponent off-balance, away from the puck, or out of the play.

Crease: A marked 8-foot by 4-foot area immediately in front of each goal.

Penalty shot: A free shot awarded to a player who has been dragged down from behind before she could take a clear shot at the net.

Power play: An offensive play used when a team outnumbers its opponents because of a penalty.

Puck: A hard rubber disk propelled across the ice by the players' sticks.

Save: A stop of a shot by a goalie by blocking or catching the puck.

Slap shot: A hard shot that is taken by drawing the stick back and swinging forcefully at the puck.

Wrist shot: A shot made without the stick blade leaving the ice.

SOCCER

Corner kick: A free kick taken by an attacking player whenever a defender last touches the ball before it completely crosses the goal line.

Goalkeeper: The player who defends the goal, and the only player allowed to handle the ball with her hands.

Header: Shooting, passing, or controlling the ball with a player's head.

Midfielder: A player who lines up in front of defenders and behind strikers. The player's role is to link the forwards and defense.

Penalty area: A 60-foot wide by 18-foot deep rectangular area in front of each goal. The only area in which a goalkeeper can use her hands.

Penalty kick: A kick awarded for any personal fouls or for intentionally handling the ball by a defending player within the penalty area. The kick is taken from the designated spot, 12 yards from the goal line in the center of the penalty area, with only the goalkeeper defending the shot.

Striker: A player for whom the team targets the ball on the attack. The player is chosen for her scoring ability.

SOFTBALL

Bunt: A soft hit resulting from the batter holding the bat out and letting the ball hit it instead of swinging the bat.

Error: A misplay by a fielder that allows a runner to reach base safely or score.

No-hitter: A game in which a pitcher or pitchers on the same team do not allow a base hit.

Perfect game: A game in which a pitcher does not allow a runner to reach base.

Sacrifice: A bunt or fly ball that allows a runner to score or advance to another base at the expense of the batter, who is out.

Shutout: A game in which a team loses without scoring a run.

Strikeout: An out made by a combination of three swings and misses at pitches or having the pitches called strikes by the umpire.

TENNIS

Backhand: One of two groundstrokes. A right-handed player uses a backhand to hit a ball that lands to the left.

Baseline: A line bounding the back end of the tennis court.

Deuce: A score in which each player or side has 40 points or 5 or more games each. Either player or side must win 2 successive points or games to win the game or set.

Forehand: The other common groundstroke. A right-handed player uses a forehand to hit a ball that lands to the right.

Groundstrokes: Shots hit from baseline to baseline in a rally.

Lob: A high-arcing shot designed to go over the head of an opponent at the net.

Match. A contest decided on the basis of victory in a specified number of sets. Women's matches are normally 2 out of 3.

Serve: A stroke that puts the ball in play.

Set: A group of six games forming one unit of a match.

Straight sets: A tennis contest in which one contestant wins every set in the match.

Tiebreaker: A sudden-death finish that is played when a set reaches 6-6. A tiebreaker is won by the player who scores 7 points first, though the player must win by 2.

Volley: A ball hit before it bounces on the surface of the court.

TRACK AND FIELD

Closing kick: A runner's last spring toward the finish line at the conclusion of a race.

Discus: A wooden disk with a metal rim weighing 2 kilograms and thrown from a 2.5-meter circle.

High jump: A vertical jump made from a running start and then over a horizontal bar supported between two upright standards.

Hurdles: Artificial barriers spaced equally on the track.

Javelin: A pointed, spear-shaped stick not less than 8.53 feet in length and 1.765 pounds in weight.

Long jump: A horizontal jump for distance, usually made with a fast short sprint and a take-off from a wooden slab 8 inches wide and 4 inches long set firmly in the ground.

Pole vault: A vertical jump made from a running start using a 12-to-16-foot pole to assist the jumper in clearing the bar.

Relay: A four-person race in which each team member runs a part of the total distance.

Shot put: a 16-pound metal sphere thrown from a circle 7 feet in diameter.

INDEX OF WOMEN ATHLETES

FOR FURTHER INFORMATION

If you want to learn more about combining sports and Christianity, check out these organizations.

Athletes in Action
P. O. Box 588
Lebanon, OH 45036
513-933-2421
Fax: 513-933-2422
Website: www.aiasports.org/aia

Fellowship of Christian Athletes
8701 Leeds Road
Kansas City, MO 64129-8755
816-921-0909
Fax: 816-921-8755
Website: www.fca.org

Athletes in Action (AIA), a ministry of Campus Crusade for Christ International, has a mission, "to reach the world for Jesus Christ through the influence of sports."

AIA uses testimonies, videos, and athletic competition to achieve its goal. The organization has produced videotapes such as *Joe Gibbs-Fourth and One, Give Me the Rock!*, highlighting NBA players, and an NFL Films video titled *Spirit of the Game*.

AIA has designed a study to help athletes apply biblical principles to every aspect of athletic competition entitled *The Principles for Athletic Competition, Practicing the Presence of God*. Lessons cover such topics as motivation, competition, fear, injury, perseverance, and self control. The organization also offers *Face to Face with Michelle Akers*, relating her story of hardship and triumph and revealing how her personal relationship with Christ provided inspiration and hope for life.

AIA men's and women's basketball teams travel the world engaging collegiate and national teams. The players present Christian testimonies to fans during halftime.

Each summer Athletes in Action offers summer camps for ages eight through high school on a 120-acre campsite outside of Cincinnati, Ohio.

The Fellowship of Christian Athletes (FCA), founded in 1954, has a mission, "to present athletes and coaches and all whom they influence, the challenge and adventure of receiving Jesus Christ as Savior and Lord, serving Him in their relationships and in the fellowship of Christ."

FCA offers summer camps around the country for seventh graders through high school. Each camper receives a one-year subscription to its magazine, *Sharing the Victory*. The magazine is also available through individual subscription.

The Fellowship of Christian Athletes sponsors "huddle groups" on campuses from junior high school through college. These groups grew from a desire to continue the FCA camping experience during the school year. Huddle groups commit to grow spiritually and reach out to others in word and deed.

If you want to find out more about sport opportunities for women, check out this organization.

Women's Sport Foundation
Eisenhower Park
East Meadow, NY 11554
516-542-4700
Fax: 516-542-4716
Website: www.womenssportfoundation.org

The Women's Sports Foundation (WSF), established in 1974, has adopted the mission, "to increase opportunities for girls and women in sports and fitness through education, advocacy, recognition and grants. The Foundation seeks to create an educated public that encourages females' participation and supports gender equality in sport."

The Foundation offers a resource center, a toll-free 800 line for women's sports information, a research library, conferences, videos, educational guides, and speaker service. The WSF operates an internship program to provide opportunities for girls and women to discover and fulfill their athletic and leadership potential. The Foundation administers and distributes over $450,000 annually to teams, programs, and individuals in the form of grants, scholarships, and awards.

ABOUT THE AUTHORS

Kathy Hillman, an avid sports fan, serves as Associate Professor and Acquisitions and Collection Development Librarian for Baylor University where she was named Outstanding Faculty in 1999. She also holds positions on the University Athletics Council and the Women's Athletic Cabinet. Kathy leads conferences and has written over fifty articles for Woman's Missionary Union, which she has served in varying capacities since 1981.

John Hillman, a CPA and authority on sports history, devotes his energies to consulting and writing. His articles have appeared in *Junior Baseball, Boys Quest,* and *Sports Collectors Digest.* John covers Central Texas sports for the *Dallas Morning News* and contributes to the religion and living sections of the *Arlington Morning News.* The Texas Association of Private and Parochial Schools (TAPPS) selected him as its 1998 Sportswriter of the Year.

Kathy and John previously authored *Devotions from the World of Sports*, a 365-day devotional book.

The Hillman's family includes two sons, Marshall and Michael, and a daughter Holly. They reside in Waco, Texas, actively involved in Columbus Avenue Baptist Church.

Kathy and John view sports as an outstanding evangelistic and outreach tool. They foresee women's participation in sports will continue to grow, but everyone should strive for greater female athletic involvement and opportunities. The Hillmans foremost believe that God should be the "main thing" in life. It's not a decision between sports and God. But if God is at the center, everything else will be balanced and in proper perspective.

I can do everything through Him who gives me strength.
Philippians 4:13

If you would like to email the Hillmans with your comments about this book, they can be reached at either kathy_hillman@baylor.edu or guardeen@aol.com